THE STRIPED BASS BOOK

BOOKS BY THE AUTHOR

Secrets of Striped Bass Fishing

Fishing from Boats

Spinfishing: The System That Does It All

The Complete Book of Saltwater Fishing

Fishing the Big Four:
Striper, Bluefish, Weakfish, and Fluke

The Complete Guide to Surf and Jetty Fishing

THE STRIPED BASS BOOK

Milt Rosko

A complete guide to catching America's unpredictable game fish

Including June Rosko's favorite striped bass recipes

BURFORD BOOKS

Dedicated to our Family

June, Linda, Joe, Bob, Kelly, Jacqueline, Jennifer, Kristine, and Kelsey

We've all fished together and enjoyed every moment

Printed in the United States of America.

10 9 8 7 6 5 4 3

Library of Congress Cataloging-in- Publication Data
Rosko, Milt.
The striped bass book / by Milt Rosko.
p. cm.
ISBN 1-58080-105-6 (pbk.)
1. Striped bass fishing. I. Title.
SH691.S7 R63 2002
799.1'7732—dc21

2002011695

Contents

G.Loomis

Acknowledgments

As I grow older, it becomes increasingly difficult to acknowledge those who have helped along the way. I cannot help but believe that in addition to a wonderful mother, and a father who introduced me to fishing at the tender age of seven, my teachers played an extremely important role in what has been a very fulfilling life.

I look back at being a youngster from a family of moderate means living in Newark, New Jersey. I attended the Newark school system from kindergarten through high school, including Lincoln School, Ivy Street Junior High, and West Side High. Throughout those 12 important years, while I may not have realized it at the time, my teachers played an extremely important role in providing me the education that would build the foundation for an exciting career and comfortable lifestyle.

It's hard to single out two individuals, but Miss Carpenter, my typing teacher, paraded up and down the aisle as we typed *asdf jkl;* for hours on end. Her encouragement and perseverance resulted in my being an A-student, the only subject for which I achieved that grade. Miss Rizzolo was the sweetest, most attractive English teacher a teenager could ask for. Firm, she often challenged my compositions on fishing, but ultimately gave me the encouragement that has lasted all these years, saying, "Keep trying, Milton, you'll eventually get it right!"

I make mention of these facts in the hope that perhaps teenagers may be reading this acknowledgment, and heed my advice to take advantage of the wonderful opportunities available to enhance their education. Doing so will provide the foundation of a most enjoyable and comfortable life.

That education helped me greatly when drafted into the marine corps during the Korean War, and in a great 45-year-long career in management at Anheuser-Busch.

Left: Surf and jetty casters have a wide assortment of tackle and lures at their disposal when they seek striped bass.

Whenever I write a book or magazine article, I'm reminded of my mentor, the late Frank Woolner, editor of the *Salt Water Sportsman.* Frank bought my first magazine article in 1953, for which I received a check for $25 and 10 copies of the magazine. I was in heaven!

Frank guided me through writing, photography, and hard-nosed fishing. Some of my most memorable moments in seeking striped bass were with him as we launched his aluminum boat from the beach at Cape Cod. Memories. They're priceless.

As I write this, my granddaughter Jennifer Basilio is studying graphic arts at Monmouth University. She's a striped bass fisherman too, often walking the beach with me during summer break. I asked Jenny to prepare the illustrations for this book, and am delighted with her efforts. I trust they'll help you in understanding the techniques that I discuss in the text. Thanks, Jenny.

My major struggle in acknowledging people who have helped me over the years is that there have been so many that it is virtually impossible to single out those who deserve and should be acknowledged for what they have done. Especially those who helped me learn how to catch striped bass!

I suspect they number in the thousands, and I've enjoyed every moment of fishing and talking striped bass with them. To all I say a sincere thank-you, and I look forward to continue learning much more from you, the nicest group of people I have ever met. Believe me, there's still more to learn in the years ahead.

It goes without saying that this book and its beautiful photography would never have been possible without the understanding, help, and dedication of June. She's the lady in my life. Indeed, it was in junior high that I met June Whitmeyer, way back in 1945. We dated, and she caught her first striped bass while we fished atop the Sea Bright rock wall on an Ed's 8 block tin squid and pork rind.

We've been married for 48 years and have two wonderful children and their spouses and four fabulous granddaughters. We've spent many days seeking the princely striper, and we hope to spend many more days, and nights, doing so. If I'm in the picture you can be sure June's the one who was handling the camera.

It's been fun, and that's what fishing should be about. My sincere thanks to all who have helped make it so.

—Milt Rosko, August 2002

Introduction

Usually, the introduction to a book tells you what it is about. I'd like to expand on that a bit, and tell you how this book came into being. Back in 1965 I wrote *Secrets of Striped Bass Fishing,* which was published by the Macmillan Company. The book was well received, considering it was my first one. It thoroughly discussed the variety of techniques that anglers might employ to catch stripers. To this day I've had striper fishermen reminisce with me about the tips they gleaned from that book and how it helped them enjoy fishing for stripers.

Macmillan and other publishers asked me to revise the work, and I pondered it on several occasions. My career at Anheuser-Busch so occupied my time that the challenge couldn't be pursued. In retirement, however, there is ample time.

It didn't take long to realize how obsolete a book can be after more than 35 years had passed. Indeed, at the time I wrote *Secrets* the scientific community called the striped bass *Roccus saxatilis.* Today the scientific name is *Morone saxatilis*! Talk about change.

I'd just finished writing *Fishing the Big Four: Striper, Bluefish, Weakfish, and Fluke* for Burford Books, when Peter Burford, the publisher, asked me to consider revising *Secrets,* especially given the resurgence of stripers and the tremendous popularity they enjoy throughout America.

Looking through *Secrets* made me more certain than ever that it's not only harder to revise a book than it is to write one, but ultimately might not result in as good a book. Simply starting fresh and writing a completely new book would be best.

After all, 35 years ago we didn't have graphite rods and reels, fluorocarbon leader material, rattle plugs, hybrid lines of fluorcarbon and nylon, laser-sharp hooks, chemically sharpened hooks, and the Circle hook phenomenon. We didn't have titanium wire, color fishfinders, and superb boats. Then there are the many new tips and techniques I employ when seeking stripers. I could go on and on. We've come farther in the last five years than most people imagine, and I said to Peter, "I'll just write a completely new book."

The book you're about to read is just that. It's a book about how to catch striped bass, how to enjoy fishing for them, how to enjoy the contemplative side of striped bass fishing and the great outdoors.

I feel it's important to tell you what the book is not. It's not about competitive fishing. It's not about killing big stripers in tournaments for the most and biggest fish. It's not about pitting one angler against another, for whatever reason. It's not about the scientific aspects of striped bass propagation. It's not an in-depth history of the striped bass.

What you *will* find is every technique that I could put into words in a cohesive and organized manner that will help you enjoy striped bass fishing. Striped bass fishing is fun. It's exciting. It's contemplative. It can become a lifelong passion.

I caught my first striper on May 16, 1946, from the rocky riprap adjacent to the Highlands Bridge spanning the Shrewsbury River in New Jersey. It was in the wee hours of the morning as an incoming tide approached slack water. The linesider made the mistake of taking a tapeworm bait fished on the bottom.

From that beginning I've traveled to and fished in many of the major waterways where stripers are found on all three coasts and inland. Often I enjoyed spectacular success, but I've had my share of days when the "skunk" flag appropriately flew from the outrigger of the *Linda June*. There were also an equal number of nights when I trekked off the beach or jetty with nary a strike. It's what striper fishing is all about. Catching sometimes becomes incidental to just getting a bass to strike. To this day I'll walk several miles of beach on a midsummer night, knowing there are only a few stripers in the area, but determined to coax a strike . . . and I often do.

During my many years of seeking the princely striper, I've experienced peaks and valleys in the fishing. Commercial overfishing depleted the stocks drastically on both the Atlantic and Pacific coasts. Fortunately, sound management of the fishery has brought the stocks back, and anglers are again enjoying fine sport.

The introduction of striped bass to many impoundments throughout the country has given many inland anglers an opportunity to fish for this great game fish. These opportunities just didn't exist when I was a youngster and beginning this lifelong challenge.

In my view the striped bass is America's favorite game fish. Thousands, perhaps a million or more anglers fish for the striped bass in salt and fresh water each season. They enjoy the challenge, respect the local fishing regulations, save a nominal catch for the table if they're so inclined, and carefully return other stripers to the water. They relish the entire spectrum of striped bass fishing.

Throughout the major chapters dealing with the various techniques to catch stripers, I've tried to keep the text very disciplined, enabling you to absorb as much factual information as possible, thus enhancing the opportunity to catch the princely striper. In the final chapter on where to find the elusive striper, I've included a lot of what I like to call personal narrative. This is lighter reading, and brings together all of the fine fishing and varied experiences my wife, June, and I have had as we've sought the striper.

June and I enjoy fish dinners several times a week, and the striper is included on many occasions. June's collected striper recipes during our travels, and created many as well. She shares them with you herein and points out that recipes evolve. Don't hesitate to experiment, adding or deleting to suit your taste.

The striped bass is a wonderful resource for recreational anglers. It is my hope the techniques I've included between these covers will enhance your skills and enable you to catch this fine game fish. Enjoy catching them, and take extra care when you release those you may not need, to ensure a fishery for future generations.

CHAPTER 1

The Far-Ranging Striped Bass

The striped bass, scientifically known as *Morone saxatilis,* is called by many names, depending on where you fish for them. *Striper* is by far the most popular name, although it's also known as rockfish, rock, squidhound, greenhead, linesider, and just plain bass in various parts of its far-reaching range. The large females of the clan are affectionately known as cows, the racy lean males as bulls, and the youngsters schoolies.

America's anglers originally fished for the striped bass in its home waters of the Atlantic and Gulf coasts. But as a result of initial stockings of fewer than 500 fingerling striped bass from the Navesink River in New Jersey during 1879 and 1881 to the waters of San Francisco Bay in California, Pacific coast anglers now enjoy a superb fishery.

They're also found in many inland impoundments where stocked fish from saltwater environs and other impoundments have adapted. Many striped bass call freshwater lakes and rivers their home, with most of these waterways ultimately finding their way to salt water. At present striped bass populations exist in the lakes and rivers of more than a score of inland states.

Some of the inland lakes cannot support a population that reproduces, for there are no rivers with current that lend themselves to reproduction. In these lakes regular stocking by the states provides a population base. It is not unreasonable to assume that in

Left: Surf anglers like June Rosko, seen here casting into the surf on a summer morning, have thousands of miles of beach from which to seek striped bass.

years to come, the princely striper may be found in the waters of all our contiguous states.

With its growing expansion into new waters and a population constantly building, the striped bass is regarded by many as America's favorite game fish. It is one of but very few species providing sport for both fresh- and saltwater anglers. It's also a very a popular table fish, with firm, tasty white meat.

The striped bass is a survivor, and adapts well to the wide range of water conditions found throughout its range. In some areas populations were once threatened as a result of industrial and agricultural pollution. As a result of strict quality regulations by both federal and state governments, the water quality of many waterways has improved dramatically, and the striped bass population has flourished.

State governments have also come to realize the tremendous positive impact the striped bass has on local economies. Anglers annually spend millions of dollars to seek this fine game fish. The striped bass is a far more valuable resource as a game fish than as a commercial harvested species. As a result many states prohibit commercial fishing.

Many charter boats sail from ports on all three coasts. The happy anglers aboard the Rainbow Runner *made a fine catch while drifting with live eels off Montauk Point, New York.*

The combination of reduced industrial and agricultural pollution, curtailment of commercial fishing, and sound fisheries management has enabled the striped bass populations throughout the country to make a substantial recovery. Coastal anglers now enjoy some of the best fishing in a century.

The Atlantic coast population has perhaps the species' longest range, from Florida's St. Johns River north to the Gulf of St. Lawrence in Canada. On the Pacific coast they're found from Los Angeles, California, on north to the Columbia River in Washington. The bulk of the Pacific population makes the waters of San Francisco Bay their home. Some wandering specimens are found even beyond the extreme ranges identified here. The Gulf populations will occasionally stray into the open reaches of the Gulf of Mexico, but for the most part are confined to the many river systems that empty into it.

Striped bass have peculiar habits, and despite intensive study by the scientific community, some of their traveling habits are still not understood. The majority of stripers have a migration pattern tied to spawning. Specifically, the populations of Albemarle Sound, the Chesapeake Bay, Hudson River, and Delaware River expand each fall as stripers move to the upper reaches of these waters for a dormant winter. Pacific populations are concentrated in San Francisco and San Pablo Bays, and move into the Sacramento and San Joaquin Rivers to spawn. A constant flow of water is essential to successful spawning, with the stripers moving upstream to find sand and gravel bottom to their liking.

Striped bass are anadromous, moving from ocean, sound, and bay waters and ascending coastal rivers to spawn. With the arrival of spring—beginning as early as February and lasting to April—spawning takes place in the fresh and brackish reaches of the Atlantic waterways. On the Pacific coast it is not unusual to see spawning activity as late as July.

Striped bass are very prolific, and females breed to the age of 14 years, with the older females producing upward of 5 million eggs. Spawning begins when the water temperature reaches 55 to 65 degrees. Within days of spawning the females and males descend the rivers and begin a migration trek that may take them 1,000 miles or more from their winter quarters.

Striped bass grow to very large size—a 125-pound female was landed from the waters of Edenton, North Carolina, in 1891. Sport-fishermen generally consider stripers in the 30- to 40-pound class a fine catch, although each season sees nominal numbers caught that exceed the half-century mark. The striped bass caught from freshwater impoundments also grow to impressive size, with fish in the 30- to 40-pound class not uncommon.

The current all-tackle record recognized by the International Game Fish Association weighed 78 pounds, 8 ounces, and was landed September 21, 1982, by Albert R. McReynolds while fishing off Atlantic City, New Jersey. Many anglers feel that with successful spawning taking place on a regular basis in rivers that had previously been subjected to pollution, the populations will continue to flourish, and in years to come there will be a resurgence of stripers that top the 50-pound mark, as was the case back in the 1950s and 1960s.

Scientific studies estimate that a 50-pound striped bass, measuring about 50 inches in length, is 17 or 18 years old. In their first two years stripers grow to 12 or 13 inches and weigh approximately ¾ pound. A 5-pounder will measure 24 inches in length. A 15-pound bass is about 30 inches. It takes seven years for a bass to grow to 36 inches and weigh 20 pounds. It grows only about 2 more inches in

Trolling is a favorite technique that Steve Ferber used to catch this 30-pound striper, netted by Pete Kazura while working a parachute jig on wire line.

length, but reaches 30 pounds by its 10th birthday. A 40-pounder will measure just around 40 inches and be 14 years old.

A concern that I have had for many years, and continue to have to this day, is the increased promotion of fishing tournaments along the coasts and inland, where the emphasis is on killing big stripers. Some contests have even gone so far as enabling teams of anglers to weigh their three or four largest fish to determine the winner.

This competitiveness could have a dire effect on the recreational fishery, as it sanctions killing big fish. I've observed many anglers get so engrossed in competing to catch the biggest that they lose all reason. Often these are the same people who would have been just as happy to keep a few small fish for the table and release the breeders. The 7- to 10-year-old fish are the prime spawners, weighing from 20 to 30 pounds and producing millions of eggs. Many of us release these larger fish, much preferring the smaller schoolies when we want a striper for the table.

Striped bass movements are unpredictable. The huge populations are dependent upon a sizable supply of forage to satisfy their appetites. Often their movements parallel those of major forage

Striped bass often move close to rock jetties and breakwaters, where forage is plentiful. Casting from jetties is demanding, exciting, and challenges the skills of anglers who relish fishing from the rock piles.

species, especially the menhaden, herring, and mackerel on the Atlantic coast; the anchovy and sardine on the Pacific; and the gizzard shad and herring in lakes and impoundments.

Water temperature also plays a role in the movement of bass. During a mild fall stripers often linger along the Atlantic coast beaches until after New Year's. There are times, however, when a cold snap in November, accompanied by coastal storms, moves the fish to winter quarters early. While stripers tolerate water temperatures from 40 to 78 degrees, their preferred temperature range is between 45 and 65 degrees.

A cold winter often results in heavy ice flowing from the upper reaches of rivers in the Northeast. This keeps the water temperature down and often results in a late spawn in the spring, for the stripers simply remain dormant until the temperature reaches their liking.

The phase of the moon, particularly the full-moon and new-moon periods, also appears to stimulate striper feeding activity. The gravitational pull of the moon causes substantially higher and lower tides during these periods, and in turn substantially stronger currents and movements of forage. Successful anglers often place

It's said that you need the dexterity of a mountain goat to fish for striped bass from slippery rock jetties. It's the favorite technique of the author, who has just landed a school striper from a coastal rock pile.

their fishing emphasis on the stage of the moon that provides peak fishing in their particular areas.

Many also use the Knight Solunar Tables, which predict major and minor solunar periods when the stripers will be most active.

All of these variables come into play when you're seeking the striper.

I can well understand why this great game fish has come to be known as "prince of the unpredictables." The more I study the striped bass, and the more I know about it, the more I realize that it's impossible to ever predict its feeding with any degree of certainty. That's what makes it such a challenge.

In the following chapters I've tried to include as much detailed information as I could muster, so that you, the reader, can absorb and put it to use on your home waters, or whenever you travel to other locations to seek this magnificent game fish.

I can't emphasize enough that my enjoyment comes from seeking the striper in a contemplative way. I love the outdoors, whether seeking the striper from the surf, climbing around a mussel-encrusted jetty, plying a rip line from a small boat, or deftly presenting a fly to a cruising bass in thin water.

Striped bass fishing has been a fulfilling, lifelong challenge for me. I honestly must say, I wish I'd at my command a book such as this one when I began, for it would have saved me countless days and nights of frustration. Then again, that was all part of the challenge, and what makes striped bass fishing so enjoyable. And that's how it should be.

CHAPTER 2

Stripers in the Surf

America's coastline features thousands of miles of foaming surf crashing to its beaches. Within its range, the striped bass loves every bit of it, for the combers expose crabs, sand bugs, and sea worms, and leave small forage fish vulnerable.

Not surprisingly, no two miles of surf are alike. Maine's surf is studded with massive boulders, while Cape Cod's is miles of beaches and sea grass, with picturesque breakers crashing on the shore. The Carolina Outer Banks have awesome surf, breaking on offshore bars that extend ½ mile or more seaward. To the north and south of San Francisco Bay there's an artistic setting of steep mountains, with intermittent sand beaches and awesome waves that have traveled the width of the Pacific.

Stripers love it all, and it never ceases to amaze me how they take comfort in feeding right in the curl of the breakers, no matter their size. They're in their environment, and fortunately for beach-based casters they present a challenge second to none. Surf casting is not for the weak of heart. It's a tough challenge, physically demanding as you walk miles of beach, often testing your skills to the limit as you cast your offering into the teeth of an onshore wind. The rewards include instant gratification at the time of the strike, but it may take hours, days, or even weeks to achieve.

SURF TACKLE

Unlike many types of striper fishing, where it's easy to be tackle-specific, you encounter such a wide range of conditions in surf fish-

Left: The author grasps the leader while landing a striper from the surf on a rough morning. Striped bass frequent thousands of miles of surf along our three coasts and provide easily accessible fishing opportunities.

ing that your tackle arsenal should include a selection of outfits to accommodate any contingencies.

I've found it best to include heavy surf, medium-weight surf, and a one-handed outfit in my rod rack. That way I'm prepared for everything from a roaring northeaster with onshore wind to surf as placid as a millpond.

Beginning with a heavy surf outfit, it's important not to select an outfit that is beyond your physical ability to handle. With each passing year I've seen longer and heavier surf rods come onto the scene, and while they may have appropriate applications, many are just overkill for seeking stripers. A rod measuring 12 or up to 14 feet, with a reel capable of holding 400 to 500 yards of line, is in my view just not viable. A person of normal physical build hasn't the capacity to maximize the power of such a massive rod. As a result the outfit becomes a handicap, resulting in shorter casts than you could achieve with an outfit of moderate weight and length.

Toward this end, I've found a graphite surf rod, rated for 15- to 20-pound-test line and measuring from 9 to 10 feet in length, even 11 feet, is well suited to the surf conditions along the Pacific beaches, the South Shore of Long Island, Cape Cod, and the rough-and-tumble surf of the Carolina Outer Banks.

Selection of a spinning or multiplying reel is matter of personal choice, with the fixed-spool reel finding favor among most anglers. With either type, the key is selecting a lightweight reel with a reasonable line capacity. After all, you're striped bass fishing, not tuna fishing, and there's no need for excess line capacity; all it does is add to the weight of the reel. While at first you may not think this important, after an hour of fishing with a too-heavy outfit, you'll find that fatigue sets in, minimizing your enjoyment.

I spool 300 yards of 15-pound-test monofilament on my heavy surf reel, although I do have a larger reel that holds the same amount of 20-pound test for casting big swimming plugs and heavy tin squids when conditions dictate. Keep in mind that 300 yards equates to 900 feet, and if a striped bass spools you of that amount of line, well, then it deserves to get away!

If you've got to settle on but a single outfit, especially for a beginner, you'll find that a medium-weight surf outfit will serve you well. Rods measuring 7 to 8 feet in overall length fit the bill nicely. I'm partial to graphite because it's lightweight, although I continue to use a few old fiberglass favorites. Here too, weight is a consideration, and the lighter the better. The majority of medium surf rods are one- or two-piece, with fixed reel seats and soft plastic grips. Many anglers now favor rods equipped with cork tape over the rod blank, for the butt and foregrip of the rod; this cuts down on the rod's overall weight.

The medium-weight rod that is rated for 15- to 20-pound-test line will usually handle lures ranging from ½ through 2 or even 3 ounces with ease. For the person of average build and physical capacity, this outfit is invariably the best choice. Toward this end, many coastal tackle shops will accommodate an angler and permit him to take a couple of rods out onto a casting field to try out. Surprisingly, the big, overgunned outfits that the shops include in their selection fall short on the casting field. This is simply because most people just can't handle the big outfits. By trying the outfit before purchasing it, you're certain to choose one ideally suited to your size and ability.

Take care to balance the reel to the rod. In the medium size range, with both spinning and multiplying reels, you'll find a good selection capable of holding 250 to 300 yards of 14- to 17-pound-test line. Select a reel that balances nicely with the rod. Many state-

Surf casters often use a surf bag to carry their gear, which gives them mobility. Plugs, leadhead jigs, and metal squids are among the surfman's favorite lures.

of-the-art reels employ graphite frames with stainless-steel gears, ball bearings, and silk-smooth drag systems.

The one-handed outfit may be spinning or popping, measuring 6½ to 7 feet in overall length and rated for 10- to 15-pound-test line. My favorite is a three-piece pack rod measuring 7 feet and rated for 10- to 14-pound line, and lures in the ½- through 1½-ounce range. I often push the rod and toss lures of up to 2 ounces when there's a stiff onshore wind.

There's a huge selection of reels available for the one-handed spinning rod. Many of the frames are made of lightweight graphite. Select a model with a large-capacity spool, enabling you to load 250 yards of 12- or 14-pound-test line. While this line is a bit heavier than recommended, I find it advantageous when tussling with a really big striper in the wash.

This particular outfit enables you to fish for hours on end without fatigue, and has the power to cast a wide range of lures. It's also capable of handling stripers of all sizes. Its only drawback is when there's really heavy surf—it's occasionally difficult to work the fish through the crashing breakers. Then patience and timing are everything. Get the fish sufficiently close that you can ease it into a particularly heavy breaker, which will place it on the beach.

TERMINAL TACKLE

When rigging terminal tackle for use with lures, it's best to include a leader between your line and the lure. The refractive index of fluorocarbon leader material, which makes it virtually invisible in the water, makes it a far better leader choice than monofilament. Most surf casters employ 20- to 30-pound-test fluorocarbon, as the leader is subjected to abrasion from the striper's jaw, sharp gill plates, and fins.

Many anglers who may be using 15-pound-test monofilament as their primary line will simply tie a surgeon's loop a couple of feet in length to the terminal end of their line. Then they'll use a surgeon's knot to tie the doubled line—which now has approximately the same diameter as the heavier leader material—to the 30-pound-test fluorocarbon. The final step is to employ a uniknot to tie a small duolock snap to the terminal end of the leader, to which your lure is attached.

Rather than using the above procedure, some anglers employ a small Spro barrel swivel between line and leader, using uniknots to connect the two. The tiny size Spro barrel swivels are an extremely strong, yet small connector.

Still another leader rig that is extremely effective is one designed for use with a teaser. Begin with a 42- to 48-inch-long piece of fluorocarbon leader material, with a small duolock snap at the end for the primary lure. Next, tie in a tiny Spro barrel swivel inside a dropper loop about 30 inches from the duolock snap. Remaining will be a tag end approximately 8 or 10 inches in length. Tie another duolock snap to this tag end, making the finished tag end for the teaser approximately 6 inches long.

With this leader you fish your primary lure at the terminal end, and off the dropper loop fish a saltwater fly or a plastic grub or plastic bait tail. The concept is that the fish is attracted to the primary lure but will often strike the smaller teaser lure instead, especially when tiny baitfish are present.

Throughout this book this teaser rig will be frequently mentioned, as I've successfully used it while vertical jigging, casting from the surf and jetties, from bridges and docks, and to surface-feeding stripers. Although I've used many styles of teasers, my favorite is a saltwater Clouser Minnow with an epoxy head, tied on a 2/0 or 3/0 stainless-steel hook.

When sand eels are plentiful I'll use a Clouser tied with brown and white bucktail, with just a trace of gold Mylar. If spearing and rainfish are the predominant baitfish chartreuse and white, with a trace of silver Mylar, produces well. Blue and white with silver Mylar is another great combination.

If there is a single rig or technique within the pages of this book that all anglers would do well to use whenever they're using lures for stripers, it is this teaser–primary lure combo. It never ceases to amaze me how many stripers I land on the teaser—sometimes doubleheaders, too. As a bonus, my surf catches on the teaser have included bluefish, fluke, weakfish, hickory shad, herring, Spanish mackerel, and little tunny. They all came as a surprise while seeking linesiders!

ACCESSORIES

After carefully selecting an appropriate outfit, the next step is to ensure that you go forth properly outfitted with accessories that will enhance your beach fishing activities. Mobility is the key, especially when lure fishing, as you're most often walking long distances. This rules out tackle boxes for your gear; they simply have no place in surf fishing. Most surf fishermen employ a shoulder bag in which to store their gear, and a wide range of sizes is available, depending on the number and selection of lures and terminal tackle you wish to carry with you. Gear belts are also popular, as these have large pockets that will accommodate a substantial amount of tackle and give you total mobility. Those surfers who fish with natural baits

Jenny Basilio, who prepared the illustrations in this book, regularly fishes from the New Jersey surf. She demonstrates the correct way to hold a striper by the lower jaw, which immobilizes it, enabling it to be unhooked and released quickly.

often tote a 5-gallon pail to the beach, which includes all their gear and doubles as a comfortable seat while waiting for a strike.

I most often simply wear an oversized fly-fishing wading vest, as it has many large pockets. By carefully selecting the lures or rigs I plan on using, I'm able to move about without a cumbersome shoulder bag or gear belt.

As a result of the wide range of surf temperatures you'll encounter when seeking stripers, there will be times when a bathing suit will be perfect attire. More often a pair of waders will be appropriate. As I've often fished in the rain, I carry a lightweight parka in the rear pocket of my fly-fishing vest, which normally would hold trout. I'm always ready for that unexpected shower or nasty onshore wind buffeting me with spray.

Included in my vest is a pair of long-nose pliers, which are invaluable when removing a deeply embedded treble hook from the jaw of a bass. Snapped to my fly vest is a retractable cable, with a nail clip on the end, which makes for ease when retying line and leader. Tucked into a pocket is a retractable tape measure, enabling me to immediately measure any species I land that has a size restriction. Also included is a small stainless-steel folding knife.

For night fishing I prefer a miner's-type headlamp, powered with four A-cell batteries. The light is designed to wear on your hat, using an elastic strap. I prefer to wear it around my neck, and have replaced the elastic strap with a web strap from a fanny pack. This enables me to easily snap it around my neck, with the light resting comfortably just beneath my jaw. This keeps both hands free while I fight a fish, leading it through crashing surf, undoing a tangle, or tying on a new rig.

LURES

A great range of lures and natural baits is available to the surf fisherman. Plugs are among the most popular surf lures, as they're made to resemble the baitfish on which stripers feed. Popping plugs, surface and deep-running swimmers, needlefish, rattle plugs, and darters annually account for many stripers. Balance the size of the plug you're using to the outfit, ranging from those weighing a mere ½ ounce to 2- to 4-ounce models measuring 8 inches in length. The big plugs are made to order when heavyweight stripers are seeking out large forage such as herring, hickory shad, mackerel, and bunkers. The smaller plugs are ideal when the dominant forage is spearing, rainfish, mullet, sand eels, and the fry of almost any fish.

You'll also find a huge variety of metal squids brought into play by beach casters. Within this general category are molded block tin squids, hammered stainless-steel jigs, chrome-plated diamond jigs, Viking-style jigs, and jigs molded of lead to replicate specific bait-fish. While the majority of these lures are in their natural tin, stainless-steel, or chrome finish, other are airbrushed in minute detail.

For striper fishing the majority of metal squids are equipped with single hooks, as opposed to trebles. Some of the hooks are fished plain, while others have surgical tube skirts in red, purple, green, or yellow. Some anglers dress their hooks with bucktail skirts, feathers, or a combination of the two. Soft plastic bait tails are also popular, and these, too, are available in a variety of colors. Pork rind strips also work well.

Metal squids range from tiny ½-ounce models on up to 3- and 4-ounces. It's important to balance the size of the lure to the outfit you're using; when they're not balanced, it becomes a hardship to fish the lure properly.

Another popular lure of the surfman is the rigged eel, which combines a lure and bait. Dead eels ranging from 6 to 16 inches in length are rigged on small metal squids designed expressly for that purpose. When cast and slowly retrieved, the metal squid's keel gives the eel a swimming action not unlike a live eel swimming along.

The final lure type in the surfman's bag is the leadhead jig. Perhaps the most basic of lures, it consists of a molded lead head with an O'Shaughnessy-style hook and eye molded into it. From that point forward the lure may be dressed with a bucktail skirt or soft plastic tail. Many of the leadheads are fished in their natural, drab lead color, which often turns mearly black when exposed to salt water. Others are painted almost every color in the rainbow. Most veteran anglers agree that it is not so much the color as the action that an angler imparts to the leadhead jig that draws strikes. For unlike plugs and metal squids, the leadhead has no swimming action as it is retrieved; it must be worked with the rod tip, causing it to dart ahead and falter, much like a wounded baitfish.

With these basic lure types you'll be well prepared for most surf situations. There are, however, still other lures that are brought into play, such as spoons, which—while effective—are difficult to cast.

Some anglers use spinnerbaits, an adaptation of a popular freshwater bass lure, and a host of other variations. The key in lure selection is to not go forth with a huge selection and attempt to try every lure in your kit during an outing. Include a couple of each type, balanced to the outfit you're using, and master their use. Quite honestly, today I carry fewer lures than ever. Those I do carry are time-proven favorites. I've mastered their use, have utmost confidence in them, and they regularly bring results.

SURF STRATEGIES

Along the majority of coastal beaches you're apt to run into three basic surf conditions. First, there'll be beaches with an abrupt drop-off, where you're in over your head just a few feet from the sand, which often occurs on either side of coastal inlets.

Then you'll find miles of gently sloping beaches, where the water gradually deepens, with no offshore bar formation.

Finally, you have an offshore series of bar formations, with the waves crashing on the bars; water of moderate depth is found in the sloughs inside the bars, and deep water in the breaks between the bars. These breaks are often called holes or channels, and are where the water crashing across the bar exits the sloughs. This is the "riptide" or "rip current" that regularly gets swimmers into trouble as they're swept seaward.

The beach formations just described are ever changing. Coastal storms regularly buffet the beach, where mountainous waves can break down sandbars, wash away sections of beach, and build up shallow points of land that extend seaward in just a matter of hours. Veteran surfmen regularly take the time to reconnoiter the beaches they plan to fish, preferably at low tide on a bright sunny day. In that way they're able to determine the beach conformation and plan their strategy should they be returning to the beach in the dead of night or at high tide.

The situation where you'll usually find the greatest opportunity is where there are bar formations and deep holes or channels. You'll find that the forage—sand eels, mullet, menhaden, rainfish, spearing, and other small bait—will congregate inside the bar, moving close to the beach to take advantage of the thin water along the sand for whatever protection it offers. By having explored the stretch of surf you plan to fish beforehand, preferably at low tide, you'll know just where the deep drops are located, where the bass may be working along the edge of the drop looking for a meal. Of particular importance is where the bars break the surf—especially in a strong onshore wind, because they break the force of the wave and enable you to effectively work your lure in the white water inside the bar, where the bass and bait are often mixing it up in the 3- to 6-foot depths.

As you work your lures inside the bars, keep alert to the movement of the current. Sometimes it'll be moving to your left as the water coming over the bar seeks an exit in a cut or break in the bar on that side. Just a few feet down the beach the reverse may happen, where the water exits to the right. It's important to be alert to this current, for if you cast straight out, the lure is often swept along so quickly that you don't have a chance to work it properly.

In this kind of situation, cast at a quartering angle, up into the current, so that the lure is swept past you during the retrieve, en-

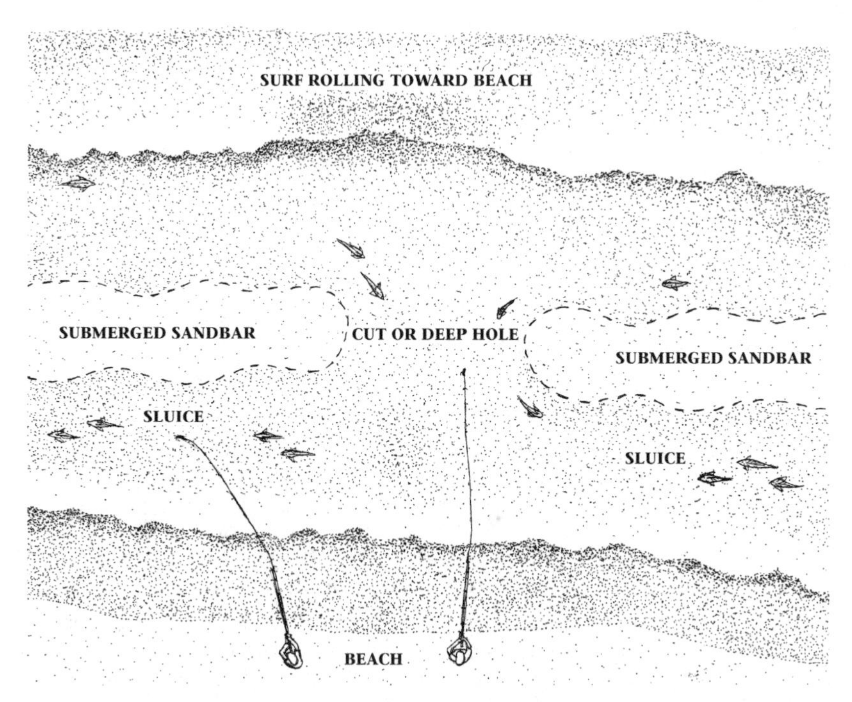

This is a typical bar formation. As the surf crashes over the bar and onto the beach, it recedes through the path of least resistance, which is the cut or hole between the bars. Stripers are often feeding outside the bar, in the cut or hole between bars, and in the shallow sluice inside the bars.

Utopia for a surf fisherman is to hook a big striper from a desolate stretch of surf. Johnny Creenan fishes along the entire Atlantic coast, seeking the prince of the unpredictables from the beautiful beaches, all easily accessible to the public.

abling you to better control its action. With this current, begin with short casts and gradually extend each succeeding cast, so that you cover all of the water with your presentation. Don't become like so many mechanical casters, casting out and retrieving for hours on end, each cast covering the same water.

Working the deep cuts often pays handsome dividends, too. Often big bass will take up station to feed on broken surf clams, crabs, and sand bugs being exposed and washed out by the current. On a dropping tide, schools of baitfish will often attempt to vacate the shallows of the slough, and rather than move out across the surf crashing on the bar, they'll make an attempt to get through the deep hole—where the bass are waiting.

Lure control is a very important consideration often overlooked by many surf casters. It begins with execution of the cast and being alert to surf conditions. With a strong onshore wind it's fruitless to time your cast so it drops into a roller crashing onto the beach—the force of the wave will continue to push it, making it virtually impossible for you to control the lure.

Instead, time your cast to go beyond a wave that is building and about to break. When it hits the water, immediately begin your retrieve if you're using a popping plug, surface-swimming plug, or needlefish. If you're using a metal squid or leadhead jig, permit it to settle into the depths before beginning the retrieve.

With each lure, you've got to learn what technique makes it work. With a popping plug, you've got to work the rod tip, causing the plug to dance, gurgle, and pop, pushing water enticingly ahead of it as it's retrieved. In the case of a surface-swimming plug an extremely slow retrieve is often best. A steady retrieve works best with most metal squids. With a leadhead jig, sometimes a slow retrieve along the bottom will brings strikes, but most often an irregular retrieve, smartly lifting your rod tip—which causes the jig to dart ahead and falter, much like a struggling baitfish—usually works best. In each instance it's a matter of finding the right retrieve technique for a particular lure.

It's important to know when *not* to use a lure as well. If you're experiencing a heavy surf, it's sometimes difficult to use a surface-swimming plug; the heavy sea pushes it about. Then a metal squid may be a far superior choice. With an offshore wind, where the surf is flat as a millpond and the water very clear, the surface-swimming plug, slowly retrieved, will bring strikes when a metal squid will be ignored.

A good rule of thumb when using a medium or heavy surf outfit in heavy surf is to keep your rod tip up as you're retrieving. This holds the line above the waves and enables you to feel and control the action of the lure, speeding up as the wave pushes the lure toward you, slowing down the retrieve as a wave recedes and pulls at it.

Always be alert to terns picking at bait. When the birds are active, it often means the bass are working bait below them. Also watch the surf for signs of nervous baitfish. Pods of mullet becoming airborne is a sign something's chasing them, and it's usually stripers. When peanut bunker are moving a couple of casts away from the beach, there's seldom anything bothering them. It's when they're tight to the beach that it pays to follow and cast your plug ahead of or to the side of the moving school. They're seeking the sanctuary of the beach, as the bass have herded them into the shallows.

With a calm surf and using a one-handed outfit, you'll often find that the stripers will work into extremely shallow water, many times chasing forage species within a couple of feet of the sand or picking up sand bugs and crabs exposed by the churning breakers. Then it's frequently effective to keep your rod tip low and pointed to the water, thus retrieving your lure so it literally swims onto the sand. Don't be surprised to receive strikes within a rod's length of where you're standing. Toward this end, it's also wise to stand back a rod's length from the edge of the water. Often anglers make the mistake of wading into the surf when it's very calm, and they're standing right where the lure should be working!

There are times when quite the opposite is true—when even though you're using a long rod and heavy metal squids, the fish are busting in bait and the gulls are screaming and diving, and you just can't get to them. It's then that wading out and punching your cast for all it's worth may reach the strike range. In the fall in particular, when the fish are migrating, I'll often carry an extra spool loaded with 12- or 14-pound-test line. I'll quickly switch from the 17- or 20-pound line I've been using to the lighter line, which sometimes gives me an additional 20 yards of distance, or enough to reach the fish.

If there's but one bit of advice I could offer, it is to be a loner on the beach. I avoid the crowds like the plague, even when a spot is hot. I like to plod along, as I find that by so doing I'll walk into pods of fish that are just moving along the beach, searching for something to eat. When your plug or metal goes swimming by, they nail it like a ton of bricks.

I should also note that when I fish daybreak and dusk, I always wear a miner's light. For me daybreak means being on the beach at least an hour before first light, for I've found the stripers to be extremely active at that time; I've often posted a good score before the crowd arrives at sunup. During the evening the fish often shut down as soon as it gets dark. There are many times, however, when the blast continues into the darkness, and my miner's light makes it easy when struggling in rough surf on a desolate stretch of beach. Oh, how I love those exhausting nights that seem to go on forever!

Once you've got the feel of a couple-of-mile stretch of beach, work it religiously. Although all that I've said earlier applies, there's a lot to be said to just getting out on the beach—day or night, high tide or low tide, east wind or west wind, rough surf and calm—and walking along and casting. Bright moon or no moon, at some point the bass will feed.

Some of the most memorable catches that I've been fortunate enough to make have occurred when I blindly walked into a school of bass. Often it was after 100 or more fruitless casts, with no bait showing in the wash and no gulls picking bait . . . just a dead-looking ocean on a desolate stretch of beach. Then suddenly the rod was practically yanked from my grasp, and the fun began. That's what midwinter memories are made of!

CHAPTER 3

Jetty Casting for Bass

Of all the ways I've sought striped bass on all three coasts and in the many impoundments in which they thrive, none is more challenging than catching this great game fish from a coastal jetty.

The many groins and jetties extending seaward along our coasts are a hostile environment to begin with. They're constructed of pilings and timbers, or strategically placed rocks that would challenge a mountain goat. At the waterline they soon become covered with mussels and slippery marine growth. Add heavy seas cascading across the jetty, swept by an onshore wind showering it with salt spray in the dark of night, and you've a picture of the platform from which you'll seek the princely striper!

There's no question in my mind that being part of the fraternity affectionately known as "jetty jockeys" gives me my greatest personal satisfaction. It's a type of fishing that I've loved dearly since I was a teenager, perhaps brought about by the element of danger, but more because of the challenge. Simply stated, none of the techniques described in this book begins to match the challenges you'll confront when jetty fishing. It requires stamina, determination, skill, and dexterity. When you land a striper from these structures that extend seaward, the experience has depended solely on your abilities, and it is indeed a challenge.

The general term *jetty* includes what are properly called groins, which are man-made structures that extend seaward. Most were built to control beach erosion, and in recent years scientists have questioned whether they've helped control erosion or enhanced it.

Left: Keep your tip low as you retrieve lures while casting from coastal jetties, as stripers are often feeding close to the rocks. Plugs, leadhead jigs, rigged eels, and metal squids are favorites of jetty jockeys.

Some groins are little more than a series of pilings, which hold in place timbers driven into the sand. Other groins are made of rock, extending hundreds of feet seaward.

Breakwaters constructed of rock, and strategically placed in bays and rivers to protect harbors, also become platforms for the jetty jockey, often enabling the caster to reach waters not otherwise accessible.

Also included within the framework of this chapter are natural rocky promontories. Of particular note are those beautiful outcroppings located along the Maine coast, where jetty techniques are used in a very rugged environment and landing a striper demands the utmost skill.

Rock jetties have been built at the mouths of most inlets along the Atlantic coast, and are designed to prevent shoaling and help maintain channel depth for the safe entry of vessels. The inlet jetties are casting platforms that require an entirely different technique than the groins do, and those techniques will be covered in depth.

JETTY SAFETY

Safety should be your primary consideration when you decide to try your hand at seeking stripers from coastal rock piles. Secure footing becomes paramount, and regular footwear is simply unacceptable—in fact, it's unsafe. The rocks, pilings, and timber on which you'll be walking are often wet, which in itself makes for slippery footing. Add a covering of slippery marine growth and footing becomes treacherous.

There are several choices available to help you securely move about the rocks. For many years jetty fishermen strapped ice-fishing creepers to their boots or waders. The pointed metal prongs of the creepers penetrated any marine growth and enabled them to move about with ease.

Innovation soon took over, as anglers became aware that aluminum-cleated golf soles were equally effective. As such, golf shoes became the preferred footwear for jetties where boots or waders weren't essential for entry. As a next step, many of us had our neighborhood shoemaker carefully remove the soles from boots and waders and cement a pair of golf soles to them. This system worked extremely well: As the aluminum golf cleats wore out, they could be removed with a special wrench designed for that purpose and replaced with new ones.

Footing is often treacherous on slippery, moss-covered rocks. Veteran jetty jockeys wear footwear with cleats to secure their footing, such as the Korkers pictured here, which are strapped to their shoes or boots.

For an angler who may not wish to modify boots or waders, an excellent alternative is a pair of Korkers. These are well-engineered pieces of footwear designed primarily with trout fishermen in mind, to secure their footing while wading swift-flowing streams filled with moss-covered rocks. Korkers comfortably fit over your boot's foot, and are held in place with secure straps. They have threaded, replaceable spikes of carbide, steel, or aluminum that secure your footing on a slippery surface.

Still another option is to obtain a pair of oversized rubbers fitted with golf soles, which can in turn be slipped over your boot's foot.

The point is this—and I must repeat it, as it's extremely important. Safety is paramount. Don't think it doesn't matter. Talk with the first-aid squads along the seacoast. Many will tell you hardly a weekend goes by that they don't have to respond to a call as a result of someone falling and being seriously injured on a coastal jetty. Usually the person paid no heed to safety, and was walking around wearing a pair of sneakers, and suffered as a result. Don't—*don't ever*—go on a jetty without safe footwear such as described here.

ACCESSORIES

For night fishing I've found a miner's headlight to be very effective, both for maneuvering on the rocks, and while playing and landing a fish. Many of these lamps are worn on the head, which I find uncomfortable. I've thus modified the straps, using webbing from a fanny pack, which has plastic snaps. I snap the light around my neck, where it rests under my chin. I'm able to tie knots, change lures, see where I'm walking, and have a clear view of a striper as I lead it to the rocks without ever having to fumble with the light, simply by moving my body.

For years I carried a gaff with a 7-foot-long bamboo handle, which enabled me to land big stripers without too much difficulty. Some states now prohibit the use of gaffs; in addition, almost all states have size limits, and it becomes tricky trying to determine if a fish is sufficiently large to use a gaff for landing. Where permitted, I still carry a gaff, but only when I'm using big lures and targeting big fish, and I only use it when it's evident the fish is well over the size limit. Otherwise I lead it either to the beach or into a pocket in the rocks, where I can grasp the leader to land it.

Because mobility is so important on a jetty, I've found that wearing a fly-fishing vest with big pockets is ideal—I can carry a good selection of lures with ease. I also carry a short length of plastic clothesline to carry fish, a retractable nail clipper for convenience when trimming line or leader, and a pair of long-nose pliers for ease in hook removal. It's also helpful to wear a hooded rain suit to keep you dry, for even in calm weather there'll often be a big sea that sneaks up on you and provides a shower of spray.

TACKLE

My preference in a casting outfit for jetty fishing falls in the intermediate range. I like to use a graphite rod measuring 7 to 8 feet in overall length, rated for lures in the 1- to 4-ounce range. This in itself tells you it's a beefy outfit with which you can pitch a lure into a stiff wind, which is when the bass are often active.

An intermediate-sized saltwater spinning or multiplying reel that can hold 250 yards of 15- or 17-pound-test line balances well with the rod, and is sufficiently light in weight that there's little fatigue when you're casting for hours. The 15- and 17-pound test line is a good compromise—it resists abrasion well, as often it'll be pushed against the rocks or slide over mussels while you're retrieving.

For the most part the one-handed casting rod and heavy-duty surf outfit have little application in jetty fishing. You'll quickly see that the great majority of strikes you receive will come within a few rod lengths of where you're standing. This is because many fish are seeking a meal close to the rocks, or striking their quarry in order to prevent it from reaching the sanctuary of the rocks.

It will quickly become apparent that the water close to the rocks is inhabited by crabs, sand bugs, lobsters, and finfish such as cunner, tautog, spearing, sand eels, rainfish, and the young of many game and food fish. Often at night you can shine a light into the water and see schools of spearing that number in the thousands. You can hear them swimming excitedly on the surface close to the rocks to avoid the stripers that are prowling just a few feet away. That's what makes jetties such an appealing platform from which to fish.

Terminal tackle for jetty fishing is essentially the same, with respect to leaders and lures, as discussed in the chapter on surf fishing. Over a span of many years I've become very selective with respect to the lures I carry with me—it's just too uncomfortable to be burdened with a surf bag weighing me down. A couple of plugs, including a surface swimmer, a subsurface swimmer, and either a rattle plug or a mirror plug are included in one pocket. A couple of tin squids, Hopkins No-Eqls, Shorties, and Avas are tucked into a compartmented canvas bag. Rounding things out is a selection of leadhead jigs. When I'm fishing regular jetties I use the smaller sizes, ranging from ½ to 1½ ounces, and move up to 2- to 3-ounce models when I'm probing the depths of coastal inlets, where the heavy weight is often required in order to get to the bottom with deep water and a swift-running current. Depending on the season of the year—and particularly during midsummer nights—I'll often carry three or four rigged eels. This is especially true if a few of the jetty regulars are scoring and big stripers are known to be in residence around the jetties I plan to fish.

JETTY STRATEGIES

In jetty fishing, as with surf fishing, it's important that you get to know the water you plan to fish. Look at almost every coastal jetty at high water, and you'll usually observe a neatly engineered structure extending seaward, just like the blueprint called for when it was built.

Arrive at the same jetty at dead low tide, however, and suddenly it's an entirely different picture, with many rocks tumbled about across the front and some single rocks scattered helter-skelter on either side, often 40 or 50 feet from the primary structure. They were no doubt unceremoniously tumbled there during a hurricane or northeaster. Suddenly you realize how important it is to know the water, where to place your casts, where the stripers are apt to be holding, and the spots to avoid for fear of hanging up your lures. Surprisingly, as you get into jetty fishing, your brain responds like a computer, calling up the files of each jetty as you approach it; the past history of good catches comes into play as you plan your strategy while climbing onto the first rock.

Each jetty, as you will quickly learn, has key spots that hold fish. I liken them to a trout stream, where tumbled boulders, eddies, and deadfalls provide relief from the swift current and trout stem the current as they wait for food to be swept their way. On a jetty the only way you can get to know just which spots produce best is to work the entire jetty.

The key is bracketing the jetty with casts, beginning as you first walk onto it. Looking left as you approach it, watch how the waves

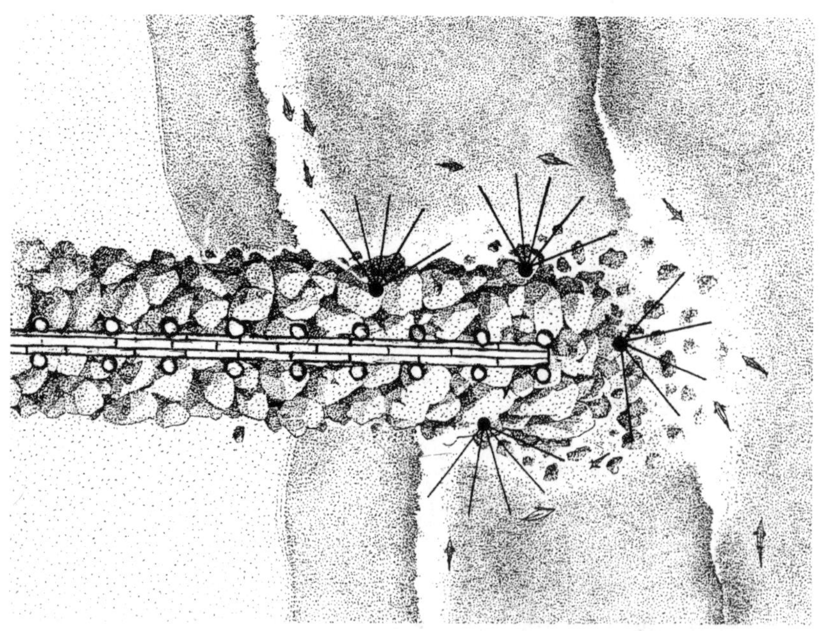

Every coastal jetty has a different configuration, and it's important to place your casts so that every inch of water is covered. Bracket the water from where you're standing, then move out farther on the jetty and bracket the water again. Often the stripers feed right in close, searching for a meal among the rocks.

are building. Position yourself as low to the water as safety permits. Begin by making your cast seaward, so your first retrieve is not quite parallel to the jetty. Always, but always, keep your rod tip low, and pointed to the water as you retrieve. You want your lure to literally swim right into the rocks, not skim across the surface, which will often happen if you hold your rod high in the air. Many anglers are so fearful of losing their lures that they keep the rod tip pointed skyward. Granted, they lose fewer lures using this approach. But they also negate the effectiveness of their lure during the most important part of the retrieve, which is when the lure is approaching the rocks, where it's the last-chance café for the striper to nail it.

Where the rocks meet the sand is often referred to as "the pocket," and it's here that bait often congregates as it moves down the beach. Baitfish are often fearful of moving around the jetty front, for they're aware that stripers are frequently there waiting for them.

After making a couple of casts and working your lure through the pocket, move out 15 or 20 feet on the jetty and make several casts parallel to the beach. Then move off, to beyond where the waves are breaking, and place a couple of casts seaward of the cresting waves. Often in this churning water, stripers are moving along the bottom looking for crabs, sand bugs, and clams exposed by the wave action.

Continue moving seaward, and always bracket the area, casting toward the beach, paralleling the jetty, then out at a 45-degree angle from where you're standing, then straight in front of you, then 45 degrees seaward, and finally seaward and almost parallel. Move out again and repeat the same procedure until you reach the end of the jetty.

Here's where the action often is, and believe me when I say it's one of the toughest spots to fish. The ravaging action of the ocean has often tumbled the rocks about, placing lots of them in front of you. Given the incoming waves, it's virtually impossible to get down in the rocks close to the water. You've got to find a rock on which you can comfortably stand to execute your casts and have a relatively clear path to retrieve your lure.

Fishing the jetty fronts often doesn't allow you the luxury of being low to the water and snaking your lure right in among the rocks. If you try to do so, the waves often push the line or lure into the rocks; all you can do is break off. Here it's best to cast out, keep your tip low, and, as the lure approaches the submerged boulders, gradually lift your rod tip, swimming the lure right over the submerged rocks.

Here you'll feel the push of the waves more than on the sides of the jetty. You should compensate for the wave action, speeding up your retrieve as the wave pushes the line and lure, slowing as the wave passes or recedes.

Over the years I've observed so many anglers who become mechanical casters when they're fishing. Cast and retrieve. Cast and retrieve. Most often there is no regard whatsoever to wave action or current pushing against their line, or whether the lure is working properly or just being dragged through the water. It's very important to have control of the lure at all times. This means through proper placement of your rod tip, most often pointed in the direction of the line, and often adjusting your retrieve speed several times during a single cast.

Each particular lure you employ requires a specific style of retrieve in order to be effective. I've found that it takes great discipline to retrieve a surface-swimming plug extremely slowly, barely turning the reel handle so the plug swims enticingly right on the surface. The same retrieve with a leadhead jig will seldom produce results, whereas using a methodical whip retrieve, causing the jig to dart ahead and falter, draws strikes. If you've ever watched a live eel swimming in the water, you will have noticed it moved in no particular hurry; that's how you should retrieve a rigged eel, so it swims with a lazy, natural movement. Experience will dictate the retrieve style that works best.

Without question the single best advice I can offer is that when you cast a lure—other than a surface plug— you must give it sufficient time to settle into the depths before beginning your retrieve. The majority of unsuccessful anglers begin their retrieve immediately. This results in their lure traveling just beneath the surface, far above where a striper may be probing around the rocks of a coastal jetty. This is especially true in the inlets where deep water is the norm.

Such inlets are often flanked by jetties that require a completely different technique for success. No two inlets are alike, but the similarities are such that a pattern of properly fishing them isn't difficult to develop. It's doubtful I've fished every inlet on the Atlantic coast, but in reviewing my log I see names like Charlestown Breachway in Rhode Island, Shinnecock Inlet on Long Island, the Shark River in Jersey, the Indian River, Delaware, and those long jetties at Ocean City, Maryland, to name but a few. I've caught many stripers from these rock piles, and from many other coastal inlets as well, using essentially the same techniques.

Worth mentioning again is the importance of not being a mechanical caster. What is important is planning a strategy that will present your lure to every inch of water flowing through the inlet. While it may sound difficult to do, it's really very simple.

Picture the inlet from an aerial perspective, and then lay a piece of graph paper on top of the inlet. You want to place your lure in every square of the graph, which covers every holding spot in the inlet where a striper may be feeding. This is important, because the bottom conformation—and the holding spots frequented by stripers as they wait for forage to be swept toward them—constantly changes. I've spoken with skin divers who've observed rocks and oyster rocks scattered on the bottom of inlets, depressions in the sand, and shoals that constantly change, along with clusters of mussel beds.

During any given stage of the tide, a striper may move from spot to spot, depending on the flow of the current. During peak flow the bass may rest in a shallow depression, or either ahead of or behind a cluster of rocks that breaks the force of the current. As the current slows at the approach of slack tide, the stripers often fan out to feed. Having stayed in deep water, many will move in close to the jetty rocks to feed on spearing, mullet, sand eels, menhaden, or other forage that seeks what little sanctuary the rocks offer.

Stripers are caught during both incoming and outgoing tides from inlet jetties. Given the choice, I much prefer outgoing water, for it tends to carry great quantities of forage seaward—the crabs, grass shrimp, and baitfish on which the stripers feed. The bass simply take up station and wait for the food to be carried to them by the ebbing tide. Often weakfish and bluefish join the bass, and you'll score with all three species.

If I had to choose but a single lure to fish inlet jetties, it would be a leadhead jig, with either a bucktail skirt and pork rind strip, or a soft plastic bait tail. I carry a variety of sizes from 1 to 3 ounces, as these weights get down fast and are easily bounced along the bottom in depths that range from 12 to 20 feet or more.

As the tide slows and the fish begin to move off the bottom, I may switch to the same surface-swimming plugs, rattle plugs and mirror plugs, and metal squids discussed earlier. Still, I often stick with the leadhead jigs, as they're a hot lure in this environment.

The technique I employ to get the leadhead jig through every one of the squares in the graph is relatively easy to master. Picture yourself standing on a jetty, as low to the water as you can comfortably and safely be. Let's assume the tide is flowing seaward on the ebb, and moving from your right to your left as you face the water.

Make your first cast about 30 to 40 feet in length, at a 45-degree angle up, into the current. As the leadhead jig touches down into the water, it will begin to settle to the bottom, along with being swept seaward by the current. Engage your reel, but do not begin to retrieve. Depending on the depth of water and weight of the jig, you'll usually feel it bounce on the bottom as it's opposite where you're standing.

Keep your line taut, and the rod tip pointed downward and in the direction the line is moving. You'll feel the jig continue to touch bottom, lift off momentarily, then bounce again as it heads seaward. As the jig approaches a position of 45 degrees to the left of where you're standing, it will lift off bottom, and you can begin a slow retrieve, often enhancing its action by twitching your rod tip, causing the jig to dart ahead and falter.

If you were to block in every graph square that the jig went through, it would follow a somewhat curved pattern, and if there was a striper holding on the bottom anywhere along its route, you'd receive a strike. Often, however, the strikes come as the jig lifts off the bottom at the end of the swing.

On your next cast, extend its distance to about 50 feet, and repeat the exact same procedure. You'll note that the longer your cast, the more you'll have to hesitate to permit the jig to reach bottom in what is usually deeper water. Then you'll have to get the feel of the bounce, sometimes relinquishing line to keep the jig bouncing, or sometimes taking up line to prevent slack from occurring.

Through the course of the tide the water depth will diminish and the tidal flow decelerates. You've got to be alert and compensate for the changes.

Continue extending the length of your casts in intervals as near to 25 feet as possible. I'll often put out casts of 150 to 200 feet in a wide, deep inlet, but always begin with short casts and extending the distance. Were you to make only make long casts, the lure would always flow along the same path, and any fish feeding between you and the lure would never get to see it.

After you've bracketed the area where you're standing with casts, then move out 40 or 50 feet on the jetty and repeat the procedure: short casts at first, gradually extended, until you're reaching out as far as you can. Always be alert as the jig lifts off bottom at the end of very long casts, for then you can often hesitate and let the current carry the jig through the water column at the end of the swing, where you'll frequently receive strikes. Here, too, lure control is important. Keep the line taut, take up slack, and retrieve slowly, adding action to the jig by working your rod tip.

Continue working seaward on the jetty at regular intervals until you reach the end. If you follow the procedure I've just outlined, your lure will have covered almost every area of bottom along the length of the inlet jetty. At some point during the span of time necessary to cover this large area, you may receive a strike. Often the strike feels like you've fouled on the bottom. The striper just swims up, engulfs the leadhead jig, and momentarily doesn't realize it's anything other than a tasty morsel. As the current pushes against the line, you'll find a tightening, as though you're hung up. You should lift back smartly with your rod tip, set the hook, and hold on!

With a combination of a strong fish and the current pushing it seaward, it's important to follow the hooked striper, especially if it's a big one, as it's difficult to work it back against the current, particularly when first hooked. What you want to do, however, is remember the exact rock from which you hooked the fish. Often other stripers will be holding in the same spot on the bottom, well out into the inlet. By returning to the same position after you've landed your fish, you can place succeeding casts into the same graph squares where the first striper was hooked.

At the seaward end of an inlet jetty, you'll encounter another set of conditions. On an ebbing tide there will be a maelstrom of rips and eddies; here stripers will often take up station and stem the tide, waiting for food to be swept their way. There's less current than in the inlet proper, and often the stripers will move throughout the entire water column, not just staying near the bottom as they most often do in the inlet proper.

The leadhead or bucktail jig continues to be a good lure choice. Cast it seaward and vary your retrieve. At first, permit the jig to settle to the bottom. Then begin a retrieve when you feel the jig is midway in the water column, and try a few retrieves right near the surface.

Block tin squids and Hopkins No-Eqls or Shorties will also produce in the rips and eddies, by working them through the entire water column. Deep-running Rat-L-Trap and MirrOlure plugs also work extremely well in this flowing water. Often you can cast downcurrent at a 45-degree angle from the seaward corner of the jetty and permit the current to carry the plug into the rips, then retrieve it back through them.

A big surface-swimming plug, especially the 7- and 8-inch-long wooden plugs with a spoonlike lip such as the Danny plug, are extremely effective when fishing an inlet jetty front. Cast out as far as you can and use an extremely slow retrieve. The plug will wobble from side to side in a lazy, swimming manner, much like a herring, mossbunker, or hickory shad swimming in the current. The strike you receive will be spectacular, as a striper zeroes in on the plug, engulfs it, and often leaps into the air, thrashing the surface to foam in the process.

I first began using big wooden surface swimmers over 50 years ago. Veteran jetty angler Clarence Hedding turned out homemade plugs on a home lathe, using red cedar. He used durable construction techniques, by drilling through the body of the plug. He then placed a treble hook on a cotter pin and pushed it through and out the top of the plug. He next placed a washer over the cotter pin where it exited at the top of the plug, carefully bending it over and securing it with a touch of solder. Crude by today's standards, but there was no way in the world that a striper could rip the hook from the plug, as often happened with the screw-eye construction of that era.

The remarkable thing about Clarence and his great plugs is that he left them in that soft red cedar finish, just like they came out of the lathe. No paint or varnish whatsoever. So much for fancy, airbrushed paint jobs. The spoonlike lip caused the plugs to swim enticingly, and we caught many a big striper on them from what was then my favorite inlet jetty, the north jetty at Manasquan Inlet, New Jersey. I loved that jetty, but it was subsequently "improved" by the Army Corps of Engineers through the addition of man-made concrete jacks, called doloses. These jacks—all 1,343 of them—locked together and stayed in place better than the granite rocks that had previously been used, and often tumbled away helter-skelter by powerful hurricanes and northeasters and their accompanying winds and waves.

This work was done in 1981, and some time later 29 corelocs were added to give further stability to the jetty. The doloses and corelocs, which each weigh several tons, did what they were intended to do: hold back the ravages of the ocean and stay in place. But they are not structures from which you can safely fish, and every year many people are injured when they attempt to fish and fall into the huge crevices.

The doloses were placed on the Point Pleasant side of the inlet as well, which at the time was my second favorite inlet jetty. So much for memories, as the Corps of Engineers did its job but forever spoiled the striper fishing from what were two of the most productive inlet jetties on the East Coast. Indeed, the fish are still there, but even a mountain goat couldn't properly fish for them. Toward this end it would certainly be warranted for the Corps to consider placing platforms with railings atop the doloses and corelocs, thus providing angling opportunities for thousands.

With the approach of slack water, from an hour before to an hour after either high or low tide, the inlet may be fished in much the same manner as any other groin or jetty that extends seaward. At that time rigged eels, subsurface-swimming plugs, popping plugs, and a variety of other striper lures may effectively be brought into play, as there is relatively little current to impact their effectiveness.

Becoming a jetty jockey, and climbing around groins and jetties, is not for the faint of heart. It's physically demanding, has an element of danger that cannot be ignored, and requires dedication and perseverance. The more you do it, the more experience you achieve. After a lifetime I still haven't mastered all the nuances of climbing around those rocks, covered with mussels and slippery marine growths, but I love every minute of it.

Nights with a heavy onshore wind, crashing waves, and stripers screaming line from your reel really get the adrenaline pumping. Wet, beat, and weary, you can't wait until tomorrow night, same jetty, hopefully same conditions, with the tide just an hour later!

CHAPTER 4

Fishing Baits for Bass

It has often been said that with the passage of time many surf and jetty anglers grow weary of casting lures, trudging along the beach, and climbing around rock piles. While I still love casting lures, there are also many times when I'll head forth with natural baits. It's a relaxing and rewarding technique that regularly produces striper catches from both rock piles and the beach.

Indeed, it was way back on May 16, 1946, that I sat on a pile of riprap adjacent to the Highlands Bridge in New Jersey and caught my first striped bass. I was bottom fishing with a tapeworm bait on an incoming tide, and I've been a believer in the effectiveness of natural baits ever since.

From early spring through late summer striped bass spend a great deal of time foraging along the bottom searching for a meal. The huge schools of fingerling mullet and peanut bunker have yet to drop out of coastal bays and rivers. That's when a meal will be easy to come by. Until then however, the linesiders continue their never-ending search for a meal, and most of the time it's something they pick off the bottom. Keep in mind that if you're a hungry striper, you spend a lot of time looking and very little time eating.

Throughout the summer I often wear a bathing suit while fishing the surf, and when the surf is down and the water is clean, I'll frequently wade out and survey the bottom. Not surprisingly,

Left: Surf fishing with natural bait is a waiting game. Knowledge of the area you plan to fish is extremely important. Most surf casters visit the area they plan to fish at low tide to determine the surf's configuration—where the bars and cuts are located—then fish the choice locations on a rising tide.

I really don't find much that a striper's apt to eat. There are sand bugs that scurry into the sand, while calico and blue crabs swim hurriedly away. After a storm there's often huge numbers of broken clams at the drop-off, which provide an easy meal. Still, most of the time there's just smooth sand bottom as I wade out up to my neck trying to find what they might be feeding on.

Striped bass foraging along the beach are often happy simply to find anything to eat. As they move along, they just gobble up whatever's available. It may be clams, crabs, sand bugs, live baitfish, or perhaps the remains of baitfish that have expired. I hold this view after having cleaned striped bass over a period of many years. I've frequently found three or four different kinds of forage in their stomachs at one time, including bunker, clam, crab, mullet, or other combinations that included sand eels, rainfish, herring, mackerel, squid, and—on rare occasions—sea worms and eels.

This isn't a habit just of Jersey stripers. I've found it true when I fished the beaches at Montauk and along the Delmarva Peninsula. Even up at Cape Cod I've always been amazed at stomach contents. Indeed, renowned surf caster Frank Daignault, in his fine book *The Trophy Striper,* sings the praises of using chunk bait to score with trophy stripers, and he's a veteran of the beach who has caught his share of heavyweights and then some.

Simply put, a hungry striper searching for dinner is apt to gobble up whatever it finds resting on the bottom, carried along by the current or tumbled over by waves crashing onto the beach. It's like a buffet table, and the fish might have a small crab, gobble up a mouthful of sand bugs, and delight in the meat of broken clams or, especially, in the remains of almost any fish it can find.

Just last summer, after a particularly strong northeaster, I decided to go to the beach after dinner. My only problem was that Ernie Wuesthof's was already closed, and my jar of brined clams was depleted. Searching the freezer, I found a box of squid. Remembering exciting catches I'd made on squid heads on the outer Cape, I pulled off the heads of half a dozen.

June and I repaired to the beach, and before I'd finished baiting my rig June's rod was arched over, and she was heading south along the sand following a frisky striper. I doubt there were many squid heads along the surf, but several bass that evening found them to their liking. I later learned, while cleaning a couple of bass, they were gorging on clam meats from the storm, along with calico crabs. Still, they wouldn't pass up an appetizer like a squid head and its eight tantalizing tentacles!

By now you should be aware that it's not what you're putting out on the buffet table, but how you're presenting it. An appetizing Swedish meatball often is more appealing than beluga caviar; likewise, a chunk of bunker or mackerel, or a lowly squid head, may be just the ticket for a hungry striper.

Because of the weight of the sinkers and baits used, most beach and jetty casters employ their medium or heavy outfits. For night fishing, many anglers equip their rod tips with tiny lights. With the rods placed in rod holders, you can readily distinguish even the lightest strike, as the light's movement is readily apparent. Generally speaking, the one-handed outfit is just a bit too light for the terminal tackle you're casting.

The ordinary 5-gallon pail has become the tackle box/live-bait container of choice for most shore-based anglers. Two pails are used when live-bait fishing, with one for tackle and gear and the other for the live baits.

Many anglers include a tool-type insert that is compartmented and fits in the pail, and is used to hold sinkers, rigs, a knife, pliers, a cutting board, bait, and a rag. Drill two 2½-inch-diameter holes in the top of the pail's cover and insert a sand spike into each, which makes it easy to carry everything to and from the beach.

On arriving on the beach, push the sand spikes deep into the sand so they can't be pulled over, positioning them not far from the bucket, so they're always in view. By placing the cover on the pail you convert it to a comfortable seat as you wait for a strike.

Many rigs can be used to present a bottom bait along the surf. The rig I observe being used most often is built around a three-way swivel, with a short drop to a pyramid sinker from one eye, a 36-inch-long leader off the other eye, and a 4/0 or 5/0 Beak- or Claw-style hook. This rig, while popular and effective, has a drawback in that during the cast the bait and leader lie back over the line, often resulting in a tangle. The rig, however, is popular and regularly accounts for many bass.

A rig that avoids this problem may be tied with ease. Begin with a 6-foot-long piece of 30- or 40-pound-test fluorocarbon leader material. Tie a small black barrel swivel to one end of the leader and a small duolock snap to the other. Approximately 6 inches from the swivel, tie in a large dropper loop that, when completed, will extend 6 or 8 inches from the remaining leader. Move down the leader 20 inches and tie in another dropper loop, the same size as the first, extending 6 or 8 inches from the leader. When laid flat, you have the swivel, 6 inches of leader, a dropper loop extending outward 6 to 8 inches, followed by 20 inches of leader, another dropper loop extending outward 6 to 8 inches, and 6 to 8 inches of leader with the duolock snap.

There are two choices to complete the rig. If you want the baits suspended 6 inches off the bottom, simply slip a Styrofoam or cork float onto the dropper loop. If you want the baits to rest on the bottom, then there's no need for the floats.

The final step in preparing the rig is to use either a Claw- or Beak-style hook with a baitholder shank and turned-down eye. If you're targeting striped bass or weakfish, a normal shank is fine, whereas if bluefish are in the area, employ the long-shank models to help prevent the blues from biting through the leader.

Slip one hook onto the loop, but do not pull it up tight; instead pass the hook through a second time. This results in a bulkiness of the leader material, which when pulled up tight holds the hook tightly in place. Were it passed through only once, the hook would have a tendency to slide up, instead of being held firmly at the end of the loop. Then repeat the same step on the remaining loop with another hook.

A sinker of your choice is then snapped onto the duolock snap. With calm surf I've often used a dipsey or bank style. When the surf is rough, I'll use a pyramid, sometimes using as much as 5 or 6 ounces to hold in the rough water.

The advantage of this rig is that the sinker is at the end of the rig; when a cast is made, the sinker moves to the target with the leader, dropper loops, and baits trailing, resulting in minimal tangles. Without floats, both baits rest on the bottom; with floats, both are suspended. Many anglers fish one of the baits without a float and the other with a float, which gives you the best of both worlds.

While you begin with a 6-foot-long piece of leader material, the final rig will measure out around 3 feet in overall length. If tied properly, the hooks on both dropper loops are sufficiently separated that they cannot tangle with each other.

In baiting up, the key is placing the bait on the hook so it stays on, both while you cast and while it tumbles around on the bottom. Use a piece of clam the size of a golf ball, leaving some of the muscle tissue hanging freely. Clams brined in kosher salt are much tougher and stay on the hook better than fresh clams, although the latter have their devotees. Using elastic thread to tie the bait firmly and securely to the hook helps keep it in place.

After a strong northeast storm I'll often repair to the beach at low tide with a 5-gallon bucket and fill it with big sea clams that the storm has exposed. I'll shuck and place them in a 1-gallon plastic mayonnaise jar—obtained from my corner delicatessen—with equal parts of fresh water and kosher salt. The brine solution hardens the clams and preserves them. The jar is placed in the refrigerator, and I've a readily available supply of excellent clam baits for several weeks.

With a squid head, just run the hook into one eye socket and out the other. As to chunk bait, cut a piece 1 to 2 inches thick and 2 to 3 inches long, depending on the size of the bunker, mullet, herring or mackerel used. A good choice is a chunk cut from the head, as this is bony. Place the hook in the lower jaw and bring it

Three of the favorite natural baits of surf casters are the head of a menhaden, the head of a squid, and a sea clam. These baits are fished on the bottom, with a pyramid sinker holding the bait in place on the bottom in a churning surf.

out the upper, which securely holds it in place. A head bait lasts longer than a center chunk: The crabs can nibble at it but find it difficult to strip from the hook because of its bony structure. The tail section also makes durable bait.

Calico and blue crabs in the shedder state, or when soft, are also excellent hook baits. If they're small you can use entire crabs, or cut them in half if they're big; in either case, secure them to the hook with elastic thread. All the baits mentioned are very durable, and many emit a scent that attracts fish searching for a meal.

Sandworms and bloodworms also prove very effective, but are very delicate bait. The preferred method of hooking a large sandworm is to insert the hook point into its mouth, thread approximately 1- inch of the worm on the hook, and exit the hook point, pushing the worm onto the shank of the hook, where the baitholder shank will hold it securely. Hooked in this fashion, the worm swill swim actively in the current. If the sandworms are small, you can insert a second worm in the same manner.

Bloodworms are usually smaller than sandworms, and many anglers thread two or three worms on the hook by inserting the hook in the center of the worm, permitting both ends to swim freely. Tapeworms are very brittle, and are best threaded onto the hook, permitting a small piece or two to hang loosely.

BAIT-FISHING STRATEGIES

When fishing natural baits, you'll encounter three basic beach formations: the gently sloping beach, the beach with a steep drop-off, and the beach with a bar formation where there are breaks between bars with deep holes separating them, and sloughs inside the bars.

With the gentle slope and steep drop-off, it's usually not too important precisely where you fish; the water is essentially the same over long distances. In these two kinds of beach formations, begin by keeping your bait right outside the heavy breakers of the first wave. If that doesn't produce, make a longer cast, which places your baits perhaps twice the distance from the beach as your initial cast. Thus, fish moving parallel to the beach are apt to intercept one set of baits, which is separated from the other by perhaps 100 feet.

The beach formation that's best is a nice bar formation with very pronounced breaks between bars, often called holes or channels (scout during the day and at low tide to determine just where they are), and nice moderately deep sloughs inside the bars. The fish will usually be feeding either outside the bar, in the deep hole between the bars, or in the sloughs inside the bars.

At low tide you can sometimes wade to the bar and fish outside it. But take care to be alert when the tide floods—you want to vacate the bar before the water gets too deep, blocking your exit to the beach. On the flood you're forced to stay on the beach, at which time it's best to fish one set of baits in the 3- to 5-foot depths usually associated with the sloughs, and another in the deep hole. This gives you a shot at fish no matter where they're moving.

The fish inside the bar often cruise right along the edge of it, as the waves crashing across it turn up crabs, sand bugs, clams, sand eels, and other fry; they just pick away at whatever is exposed. Sometimes on a sunny, clear day you can see the fish, often working in water just a couple of feet deep.

When fishing the surf, or from adjacent jetties, with natural bait on the bottom, you've got to have patience. There are times when the first cast brings a strike—but many other times you may have to wait for hours before that strike. When you do hook a fish, always keep in mind that they're often traveling in pods, and they're not going to hang around long. Don't fiddle-faddle. Unhook the fish, either keep or release it, bait up, and get that line back in the water quickly, for often you'll promptly be rewarded with another strike.

Talk with almost any skin diver and you'll quickly learn there's a population of stripers in permanent summer residence among the submerged, tumbled rocks on the seaward ends of most groins and jetties. Many are caught on dead bait, but few will dispute that a live bait is an almost certain way to success.

While a jetty or groin is an excellent casting platform, make certain to position your baits, either dead baits on the bottom or live baits swimming about, so they're in a position to be intercepted by stripers feeding around the rocks. Many anglers make the mistake of casting their baits too far from the jetty, failing to realize that often the bass are cruising within 50 feet of where they're standing. These bass are seeking the forage that is in tight to the rocks, which provide limited sanctuary from the predators.

FISHING LIVE BAITS

The scientific community tells us that a hooked baitfish sends out signals of distress, which are readily picked up by other fish. It's said that fish otherwise content with a full stomach will immediately search out the source of those signals. Indeed, I'm a believer, as I've caught many big stripers that have had as many as four to six adult menhaden in their stomachs. I often wondered where they were going to put the one they struck!

While live bunkers have long been the bait of choice when fishing from rock piles and beaches, you can enjoy extraordinary success with live herring netted from flumes emptying into the ocean. You can also score with live anchovies, mackerel, spot, croaker, and snapper bluefish. For years many anglers employed small winter flounder, blackfish, and scup as bait, but in many states there are size restrictions and seasons on these species, and it is a violation of regulations to use them as bait.

Often just catching the bait can be lots of fun. Among the most enjoyable is catching live sea herring and hickory shad on Clouser teasers or shad darts, and then immediately placing them on a hook and scoring with bass.

Not to be forgotten is the lowly common eel, perhaps the best natural striped bass bait of all, and the easiest to keep alive, on the hook, and cast with ease. Eels from 6 to 18 inches long make ideal

This is a typical gently sloping beach, where the waves crest and break right onto the sand, without a bar formation. Often the stripers move in very close to the beach to feed. Alternate your casts, some far off, some close, until you find where the stripers are feeding.

baits. Over a period of many years live eels—and dead rigged eels—have produced extremely well for me at most of the renowned striped bass hot spots from the Chesapeake Bay to Maine. Surprisingly, of the many stripers I've cleaned, I've found very few eels in their stomachs.

The most convenient way of transporting live baits to surf and jetty locations is via a 5-gallon pail three-quarters filled with seawater. Carry only a couple of baits at a time—the oxygen in the water will last longer, and the baits will stay livelier. Don't make the mistake of putting four or five baits in a bucket, as they'll quickly deplete the oxygen and before you may even realize it, they'll expire.

For fishing live baits, you can achieve better control using a multiplying reel than with a spinning. A 7- to 9-foot-long rod rated for 20-pound-test line will handle even the heaviest live baits with ease.

Those who prefer livelining most often employ a 36- to 48-inch-long 30-pound-test fluorocarbon leader. Fluorocarbon's refractive index makes it virtually invisible in the water. The leader is tied to the line by first using a surgeon's loop to double the last foot or two of your terminal line, and then using surgeon's knot to join the double line and leader.

The hook, most often a size 5/0 or 6/0 Claw, Beak, O'Shaughnessy, or 12/0 Circle style, is tied to the end of the leader using a uniknot. You can also employ a treble hook with live bait, using one of the three hooks to impale the bait, with the remaining two hooks in position to penetrate once a fish inhales the bait. Gaining popularity with live-bait fishermen are the new Mustad Triple Grip trebles in 3/0 size for medium-sized baits.

The conditions will often determine just how you should hook the live bait for livelining purposes. If in an inlet with outgoing tide, where there is a swift current, it's advantageous to hook the baitfish so that it can swim effectively and appear to be stemming the tide or current. This is best accomplished by placing the hook through the lower jaw and out the upper, through the eye sockets, or through the skin above the eyes.

If, however, you're casting from the surf or jetty, where there is minimal current, and you wish the baitfish to swim away from the structure, then it is appropriate to place the hook in the back of the baitfish between the dorsal fin and tail. This enables the baitfish to swim away from the structure unimpeded, and requires minimal casting.

Using this technique, a caster will often pull back gently as the baitfish attempts to swim away, encouraging the baitfish to become more aggressive and swim away from the structure—which is what you want it to do. This approach works particularly well when using live menhaden, hickory shad, herring, mackerel, and eels.

When using live bait, you'll find that the bait will often settle into a pattern of leisurely swimming about, unconcerned that it is, in fact, on a hook. When approached by a big striper, the bunker, mackerel, hickory shad, or other baitfish will excitedly swim about at an accelerated rate of speed, often breaking the water as it attempts to elude.

This is when you need patience. Big stripers will often toy with the bait, watching it and circling before ultimately making a decision to engulf it. You've got to keep your reel in free spool, permitting the bait to swim freely, unimpeded. Once the fish has taken the bait and moved off, it's wise to hesitate, and hesitate some more, for at least a 10-count. Then, with the rod pointed in the direction the line is moving, lock the reel in gear and lift back smartly to set the hook. If you've timed it correctly, the rod will be practically ripped from your hands as the lunker moves off.

A rather unique technique for presenting the big live bait from shore, pier, or jetty is to use what is popularly referred to as a "breeches buoy rig." This rig uses the same principle as a breeches buoy, moving an object from one place to another on a line, using the angle of descent, coupled with the weight of the object, as the propellant.

To prepare a breeches buoy rig, begin by tying a duolock snap directly to the end of your line using a uniknot. For this type of fishing 30-pound-test line is preferred, as there is some additional friction and pressure on the line. Then snap on a pyramid-style sinker.

To make up the leader, begin with a 24- to 30-inch-long piece of 30-pound-test fluorocarbon. Tie a combination barrel swivel and coastlock snap to one end of the leader and your hook of choice to the other.

Bait up the hook as discussed earlier. The method of choice for this type of rig is placing the hook in the fleshy part of the back either before or behind the dorsal fin, enabling the fish to swim about unimpeded.

The next step may sound unusual. Determine where you want the bait to be and cast your sinker to that spot, without any rig attached whatsoever. The final step is to open the coastlock snap attached to the leader, place it around the line between the tip of your rod and the sinker—which may be 150 feet or more away—and snap the coastlock snap shut. Lift the rod tip into the air and pull the line taut, while releasing the fish attached to the breeches buoy leader rig. It will gently slide down into the water.

I first used this rig many years ago while fishing for king mackerel off Florida piers. My first time using it in Jersey dates back many years, too. It was off the top of the Sea Bright rock wall. It was a neat way to get the bunker out 150 feet or more from the rocks. Just snap it onto the line and away it goes! Importantly, on the very

A breeches buoy rig is an effective way of presenting a live bait far from where you're standing on a beach or jetty. A coastlock or duolock snap is tied directly to the end of your line, and a pyramid sinker snapped to it. The sinker is then cast. The leader is made up of a coastlock or duolock snap and swivel, tied to a 3-foot-long piece of 30-pound-test fluorocarbon, and a 5/0 or 6/0 Claw- or Beak-style hook. A live baitfish is hooked through the lips. The snap is opened and slipped over the line and closed. The rig then slides down into the water, where the baitfish is able to move about freely.

first day I tried it, with a couple of live bunkers purchased at Bahr's Landing in Highlands, I landed a pair of stripers in the teens.

As soon as it enters the water, the baitfish will begin swimming about vigorously. It can swim all the way to the end of the line, where it meets the sinker, or it can simply swim back and forth along the length of the line that is in the water. Sometimes it will excitedly swim about where the line enters the water, making a surface commotion that often attracts predators to it.

When it is not in view, you can feel that it's still there by maintaining a taut line, feeling the vibrations as the baitfish moves about. Sometimes it's wise to provide some slack line, permitting the line to settle horizontally to the bottom, with the baitfish moving back and forth along the bottom. Then, when you pull the line taut again, the baitfish will feel the pressure and excitedly begin to move about.

As a striper picks up the bait and moves off with it, there's a possibility you may hardly feel the movement, particularly if it moves in the direction the line is pointed. Once it gets to the end, and the coastlock snap comes up tight against the duolock snap and sinker, you'll get a jolt that often startles you, especially if you haven't had a strike for hours. Toward this end, it's wise to keep the reel locked in gear with a moderate drag setting, for when it comes taut the fish usually has already taken the bait well into its mouth, and quite often has already hooked itself.

This method is extremely effective, even with small baitfish. Often during the fall of the year, when huge schools of rainfish, mullet, and peanut bunker are moving along the beach, it's possible to snag them using a weighted treble hook or the treble hooks of a plug as it is yanked through a tightly packed school.

Here the effective technique is to snag a 5- or 6-inch-long baitfish, place it on the breeches buoy rig, and position it just beyond where the school of baitfish is herded tight to the beach. The struggling baitfish, off by itself away from the school, generally results in an immediate strike: Stripers often regroup away from the main school they are stalking, and find an unsuspecting single fish an easy target.

Sometimes you need only use a snag rig to snag the bait; once it's hooked, simply stop reeling and let it swim about. Often a hungry bass will find and be onto it in a flash.

As noted earlier, patience is the key. Bait fishing from beach and jetty is relaxing, and you've plenty of time to commune with nature. The rewards will often surprise you, for seldom will a hungry striper pass up a tidy offering cast just beyond the breakers.

Casting from the surf with natural bait requires patience, as is demonstrated here by June Rosko. Those who wait for a hungry striper to find their bait often have patience rewarded.

CHAPTER 5

Fishing Docks and Bridges

Wherever striped bass roam along the seacoast, you're certain to find an abundance of docks, bridges, and piers. All these structures are held in place by either pilings, caissons or other support driven into the bottom of the rivers, bays, and estuaries where they're located.

While abovewater structure provides a platform for striper anglers, it's what's down in the depths that attracts the targeted species—almost always looking for a meal. Of all the places stripers frequent, they so often choose to take up station around docks, bridges, and piers because they've come to know that at a specific stage of the tide a meal will be close at hand. Importantly, as the forage is carried with current, or takes up position in the rips and eddies created when the water swirls past the piles, the striper can leisurely wait for a meal to be carried within range.

Stripers often move great distances in the course of a day to take up station where they can easily satisfy their appetites. They prefer to do so where they can expend as little energy as possible. As such, they'll often position themselves either ahead of or behind a single piling or massive caisson. For as the flow of water, caused by tidal flow or strong winds, approaches, it separates just before and joins just after the structure, leaving a dead spot where there is very little current. The bass take up position, knowing that shrimp, crabs, squid, sea worms, or any of a variety of forage species such as spearing, mullet, menhaden, or sand eels will be soon to arrive.

Left: Milt Rosko regularly fishes back bay, river, and marina waters from docks and bridges. Casting leadhead and bucktail jigs to the shadow line often produces school stripers like the beauty he's just landed.

Still another attraction of docks, bridges, and piers occurs at night, when almost all such structures are illuminated. The bright lights shine on the water and attract myriad forage. Indeed, where during the day you'll find nary a spearing around a dock, as soon as the sun drops over the horizon and the lights go on, suddenly there are thousands of the tiny baitfish in a tightly packed school beneath the lights, with the stripers not far behind.

Stripers also have a habit of taking up station along the shadow line caused by the lights from the structure. As they do so, they'll put their nose right on the line with their bodies in the darkness as they face the brightly illuminated water, the current moving toward them. At other times they'll face into the dark water as the current moves toward them. In each instance the shadow line becomes their holding point, depending on which side of the structure it's situated.

Not surprisingly, wherever you fish along the striper seacoast you'll find a cadre of striper fanatics who fish almost exclusively from the structures. Dick Wood, an old friend from Ocean City, New Jersey, who in his youth climbed around coastal rock piles with ease, now enjoys fishing the myriad bridges that span the coastal bays of south Jersey. He's so adept at coaxing strikes from the linesiders that reside along the shadow line it's seldom he ventures anywhere else!

TACKLE

The tackle you employ while casting from a small boat or the beach will often serve you equally well as you cast from bridge railings or dockside planking. Spinning or conventional—it's a matter of personal choice. Choose a graphite rod measuring 6½ to 7 feet in overall length, with a light- or medium-weight reel that'll hold a couple of hundred yards of 12-pound-test line. Lean more toward light than heavy, as most of the time you'll be tangling with schoolies.

I'll usually employ a teaser ahead of my primary lure, and use the leader combination described in the surf chapter. I double the last foot or so of line using a surgeon's knot, and then tie the double line to the barrel swivel with a uniknot. With this combination I can use any one of a variety of lures, with the teaser an added attraction that often catches more stripers than the primary lure.

There are a great many lures you can employ from these structures. If I had to choose but a single one, though, it would be a bucktail jig, or the modern-day counterpart of a leadhead jig with a soft plastic tail. Not surprisingly, the first article I ever wrote dealt with the versatile bucktail jig and was published by *Salt Water Sportsman* magazine way back in 1954. The lure was extremely effective then, and continues to regularly account for many fine catches all along the coast.

For most bridge and dock casting, you'll find that a selection of bucktail or leadhead jigs in the ½- through 1-ounce size will work nicely for most tidal conditions. These are molded around O'Shaughnessy-style hooks ranging in size from 1/0 through 7/0. The favorite bucktail skirts are white or yellow, with the heads painted any one of a variety of colors, including red and white, yellow, chartreuse, or blue and white. The lead heads of the jigs come in a variety of shapes, including lima bean, torpedo, and many exotic models, complete with beaded eyes and detailed airbrush painting.

Leadhead jigs with which soft plastic bait tails are used are often unpainted. They're used with tails measuring 3 to 6 inches in

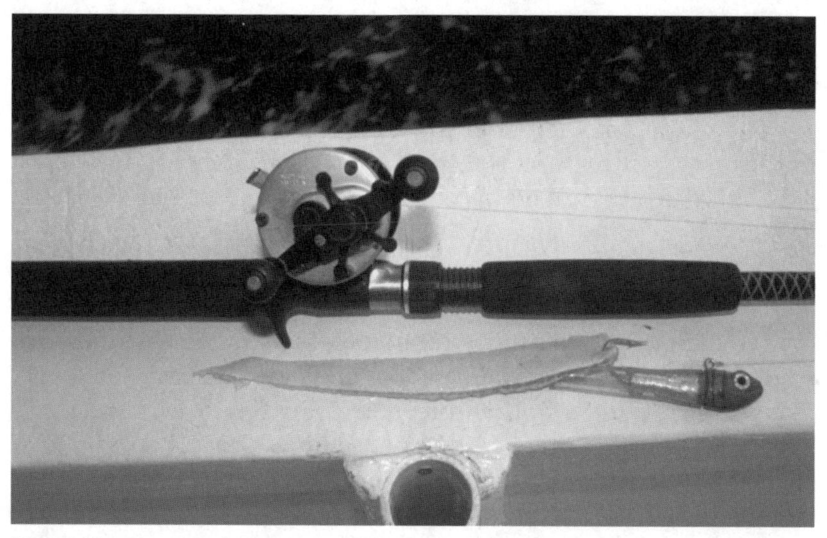

Most bridge casters prefer to use a popping outfit. A favorite lure is a heavy leadhead jig with a strip of pork rind, squid, or strip bait. It is cast up into, or across, the current, permitted to settle, and then worked back to the shadow line of the bridge lights on a night tide.

length and in a variety of colors that resemble the baitfish found in the waters you plan to fish. Some of the bait tails are exact replicas of common forage such as sand eels, mullet, mackerel, or menhaden, and their soft, fluttering tails make them appear very lifelike in the water.

Adding a strip of pork rind to the hook, which results in an additional lifelike fluttering action as the lure is retrieved, often enhances the action of both a bucktail jig and a leadhead with plastic tail.

Plugs are also extremely effective when cast from docks, bridges, and piers. Especially popular are the surface- and subsurface-swimming plugs in 4- to 6-inch-long models. Mirror plugs in the medium- and deep-running styles are also effective when probing the depths surrounding these structures. On occasion a popping plug will score, as will a darter.

Metal squids, including block tin squids and hammered stainless-steel jigs, occasionally will score. However, their design generally lends them to being most effective where there is less of a current than you'll find around structure.

Natural baits—live forage species such as menhaden, mackerel, mullet, and herring—may also be effectively drifted from piers, bridges, and docks. Sandworms, bloodworms, blue crabs, calico crabs, and squid also tempt strikes from stripers as you drift them through a rip or eddy.

The tackle and techniques just described apply to the myriad low bridges that span coastal bays, creeks, and rivers, as well as to local docks where stripers can be landed from the structure, or by walking them to the shore adjacent to the structure.

FISHING HIGH BRIDGES

Scattered along the coast are numerous high spans where casters work their lures 30 feet or more above the water, no easy challenge. Many use very stiff graphite rods measuring 8 or 9 feet in length, with level-wind casting reels loaded with 80-pound-test braided Spectra line. Their lures include 2½- to 4-ounce leadhead jigs, with large 5- to 7-inch-long plastic bait tails or long strips of pork rind.

As with all striper fishing, mastering the use of this specialized tackle from structures that are extremely difficult to fish off presents a major challenge. With this gear anglers artfully present their heavy lures, using the swift current to bounce them on the bottom.

They can free their leadheads from bottom snags with strong yet fine-diameter line. But the real purpose of the heavy gear is to enable them to literally reel 5- to 7-pound stripers—some even reel 15-pounders—right over the rail!

Many employ a snatch-gaff, rigged with three to five gaff hooks. Tied to a length of ⅛-inch cord, the snatch-gaff is lowered into the water and positioned beneath the fish; a hard yank impales it. Exercise care before using this technique, as some states prohibit gaffing stripers due to size restrictions.

Without question the most important consideration when fishing from structures such as these is having an intimate knowledge of the tidal flow and currents that surround them. Each structure will have varying flows of water during the course of a tide, ranging from dead slack shortly after both high and low tide, to raging maelstroms during the peak period of tidal flow.

FINDING FISH

Stripers will seldom be at one particular location in relation to a structure throughout the tide. They'll move about, taking up station along a shadow line as the current begins to slow. Often they will have moved out of a dead spot where they could expend little energy during the height of the tidal flow. Sometimes they'll be resting in a shallow depression along the bottom, where the heavy water flows over them, yet they remain outside the swift current that would otherwise expend their energy.

From the *Linda June* I've often probed the waters adjacent to the bridges, docks, and piers from which I fish while carefully monitoring the electronic fishfinder. I frequently find these areas completely devoid of fish, only to return hours later—usually after the tidal flow has moderated—to find the screen illuminated with stripers that have taken up station to feed.

I carefully note these optimum periods in my log, which has ultimately saved me countless hours of working water that would be devoid of fish life. Of course, other variables often came into play. The T docks of marinas that produce under the lights on night tides are often completely devoid of activity during the day, when boat traffic is constantly in the area. The same holds true around the channels funneling through bridges, where daytime activity of pleasure craft throws up constant wakes while night tides are peaceful and quiet, and the stripers take up residence.

A good rule of thumb is to recognize that at the height of water flow, the fish will either not be there at all, or they'll be in spots where they can expend minimal energy. As the tidal flow—or the flow of water caused by strong winds—moderates, the fish will begin moving about, often fanning out throughout the entire area during slack water.

Most bridges, docks, and piers are located where there is deep water in relation to the surrounding areas. My experience has been that on a flooding tide, the fish tend to fan out more in search of food. As the tide ebbs, particularly during the bottom of an outgoing tide, the surrounding flats, adjacent to the channels, docks, and bridges, sometimes lose all their water, forcing grass shrimp, crabs, spearing, menhaden, and other forage into the deeper water. Thus, the opportunity of having both stripers and forage herded together often occurs during the last several hours of the ebb, as the water is just leisurely sliding along.

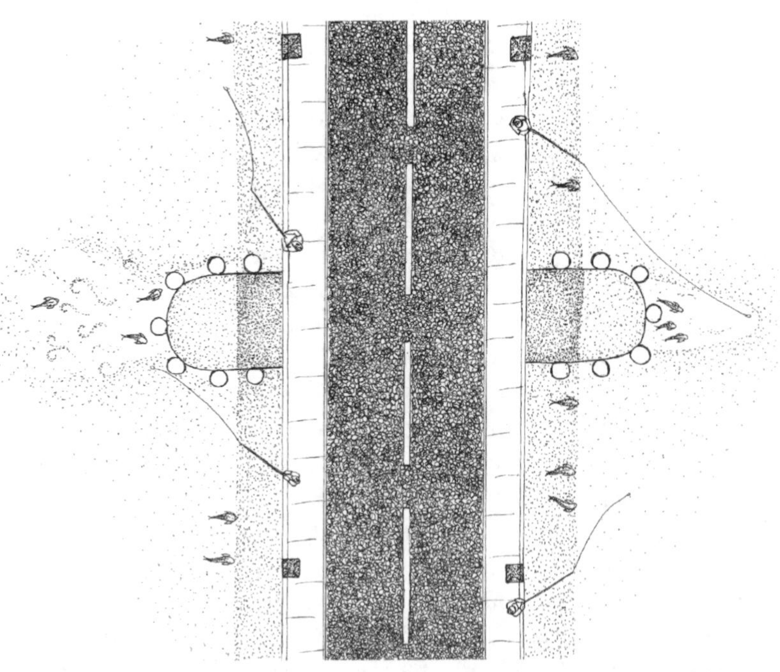

Night fishermen regularly make fine catches of stripers all along the coast by fishing the shadow line caused by bridge lights. Often the stripers take position along the shadow line, waiting for forage fish, shrimp, crabs, and sea worms to be swept toward them. Often you can see the stripers from the bridge, as they stem the tide just beneath the surface. Place your casts to present your lures within their range of vision.

In many areas the remains of old bridges are not removed, and stripers take up station to feed. They prefer the areas ahead of and behind the abutments, as they can stem the tide in the quieter water, expending less energy.

This should not be construed as a hard-and-fast rule, for you're certain to encounter times when blitz fishing will occur at the top of the tide. It is, however, important that you reconnoiter each area you plan to fish, and be alert to the activity you experience. Then on future ventures you can capitalize on that experience. Indeed, I've fished bridges and docks in many places where I could almost set my watch by when the stripers would show up at the shadow line on a particular stage of the tide.

When using leadhead jigs or plugs from these structures, you'll be presenting the lure in one or two basic ways. You might be casting up into the flow of the current, and retrieving the lure much the same as a forage species would swim along with the tide. Or you could be casting down with the flow of the current and retrieving against it much like a forage species struggling to hold position in the current or an eddy.

When casting a plug or leadhead up into the current flow, the lure will be swept back toward you as soon as it touches down in the water. With a surface-swimming plug it's important to immediately begin your retrieve, and reel at a speed that keeps your lure moving faster than the current is pushing it along. If you retrieve too slowly, the plug will slide along much like a piece of wood, with no action.

Quite the opposite is true when you're casting with the flow of the current. In this situation the current is pushing against the lure, and in some instances it's not necessary to retrieve at all, for the current pushing against the lip of the plug will cause it to swim feverishly. You then can retrieve slowly, resulting in the plug moving forward at a very slow speed. Another option is walking back and forth along the dock, bridge, or pier rail, sort of "walking the dog," with the plug swimming enticingly as you move back and forth.

The key in using any lure is ensuring that it replicates the baitfish that are apt to be in the area. Thus it's important to be alert, and not be a mechanical cast-and-retrieve individual. Make the plug work for you and you'll score.

There are times when it's beneficial to quarter the current, casting from your position at a 45-degree angle; as the plug touches down, begin a retrieve that causes it to swim across the current. It's surprising how at times the fish will respond to the lure swimming with or against the current, where on other occasions the quartering retrieve brings explosive strikes.

When you're fishing at night, there's often a pronounced shadow line from the lights of the bridge or—on a clear night with a full moon—from the moon. In each instance the stripers respond the same way, keeping their nose tight to the shadow line as they wait for a meal to be swept their way.

From spans that are low to the water, it's not at all unusual to just walk along the railing, carefully observing the shadow line, and spot individual stripers or sometimes groups of them side by side, all facing into the current. Nothing quite beats the adrenaline rush of making a cast up into the current, retrieving a surface-swimming plug back toward the shadow line, and having several stripers dart out to assault it. First one there wins!

Bucktail jigs and leadhead jigs by their very design are most effective when used to probe the depths from bridges and docks. When you're casting into the current flow, it's important to do the opposite of what you'd normally do with a plug: As the jig enters the water, hesitate and let it settle. This is where it's important to know the water you're fishing, particularly with respect to depth.

While often the fish may be holding on the shadow line at night, they're just as frequently moving about through the water column. At the height of the tidal flow they may be hugging the bottom, which means you've got to hesitate for a long count, permitting the jig to settle directly to the bottom. As the leadhead bounces bottom, lift your rod tip smartly— causing the jig to lift off the bottom—and begin your retrieve. This results in the jig moving a couple of feet off the bottom, faltering, and beginning to settle again. When it touches down again, repeat the process until the jig is directly perpendicular to where you're standing. Then reel it back up on the structure and make another cast.

If the spot has a water depth of 15 or 20 feet, then it's important to work the leadhead through the midrange of the water column. This is accomplished by timing your retrieve to begin when the lure settles to intermediate depth. Alternate your retrieves: First use a whip retrieve, lifting your rod tip smartly to cause the jig to dart ahead and falter, much like a baitfish struggling in the current. Then, on the next cast, try a slow retrieve, with just enough speed to keep the lure moving faster than it would were the current alone carrying it.

There are times when you can employ a ¼- or ½-ounce bucktail jig and work it high in the water column. Use the same technique as you would with a plug, either casting directly up into the flow of the current, or quartering your casts at an angle, and promptly beginning your retrieve. As long as you maintain sufficient speed you can usually retrieve the light lure to within a couple of feet of the surface.

On the downcurrent flow of the dock or bridge, a different approach is required. You can cast out and permit the leadhead to settle, and then work it back to the structure with a whip retrieve, much like a struggling baitfish stemming the tide or trying to make headway against it.

By far the most effective approach I've used is to cast parallel to the span, or out and across the current if I'm fishing from a pier. As the jig enters the water, let it settle to the bottom and bounce with the current. You can feel it touch down, and the current will push against the line and cause it to lift off, then bounce again, as it moves downcurrent. Many casters prefer to use a conventional reel, thumbing the line and relinquishing it as the jig bounces along, which gives them better control and lets the jig bounce bottom for a longer period, working well back into the rips and eddies.

On the downcurrent flow of the structure, you'll find that much the same logic holds true: The fish will be holding as they do on the upcurrent side. When the current is roaring the fish will avoid the swiftest water, moving about more as the current moderates.

The slack-water period—or the time an hour before or an hour after it—is when the stripers are often most active. This is when it's important to be totally mobile and move about a lot, for as the fish search for a meal you just never know where they'll be apt to strike your plug or leadhead. If you like to fish from docks, don't hesitate to move from one marina to another.

Over the span of many years I've fished from the T's of gas docks at marinas, often walking from dock to dock, and then back to the original dock, covering four or five in a few hours' time. Often I'd experience nary a hit. Suddenly I'd walk into a maelstrom of baitfish forced into the air by stripers attacking from below, at a dock where not a sign of life was present just an hour earlier.

Much the same is true when fishing from bridges. Often the ebbing tide produces good action as both the stripers and forage vacate the flats. But when the tide floods, the reverse happens, and often it's wise to walk toward the bank. Where sand flats may have been exposed earlier, it often pays to probe the shallows with a few casts as the water surges back in. For it's on the flood that the grass shrimp, spearing, crabs, and other forage move toward the bank, where the shoreline is often covered with marsh grass and provides them sanctuary.

FISHING TEASERS

Over a period of many years I've shared teaser techniques with many anglers. The single thing that most surprises the majority of them is that while their presentation centers on the primary lure, be it a plug or leadhead jig, the lure that often receives the strike is the teaser!

I've been using teasers for over half a century and attribute much of my success to them, whether I'm fishing from a bridge or dock, as discussed here, or a boat or beach, particularly with school fish. Even in their days of plenty, many large bass have been enticed to that tantalizing teaser swimming ahead of the primary lure.

Of late I've become partial to a Clouser Minnow saltwater fly with an epoxy head as a teaser. Tied on either a 2/0 or 3/0 hook, the design of the Clouser is such that when it's retrieved, its weight holds it away from the leader. Thus, when a striper approaches and engulfs it, there is little likelihood that the fish will miss the fly because it's close to or twisted around the leader.

The Clouser is tied with colors and materials to resemble every baitfish that swims in the ocean. I've settled with a few that have served me well over the years, including brown and white with a trace of gold Mylar when sand eels are in residence, chartreuse and white with silver Mylar when spearing are plentiful, and blue and white with silver Mylar when mullet, bunker, or other small forage is plentiful.

When you watch a Clouser teaser being retrieved, you'll find that it tends to ride above the primary lure's leader when using a leadhead or bucktail jig. When the primary lure is a surface-swimming plug, the Clouser will hang and swim ahead of and beneath the primary leader.

This is not to imply that other teasers are not as effective. It's just a matter of personal preference and what you have confidence in. I've used Lefty's Deceivers, Honey and Platinum Blondes, bunker patterns, and a wide variety of flies tied to imitate the forage species that's most plentiful. In fact, if my memory serves me correctly, the first teaser on which I caught a striper consisted of a tuft of white bucktail tied to a 3/0 O'Shaughnessy hook with red thread.

Soft plastic teasers are also very effective. The 3- to 4-inch-long models, when threaded on a 2/0 hook, are deadly at times. The soft plastic replicas of sand eels, spearing, mackerel, and a host of other forage species readily bring strikes as they swim along ahead of a primary lure.

NATURALS

When a teenager I was awestruck by the striper-catching ability of "Tony the fireman." Tony DeLibero was a fireman from Newark, New Jersey, and he spent countless hours on the railroad trestle that spanned the Shrewsbury River at Highlands. Tony liked to fish with sea worms, and walking back and forth the substantial length of the trestle.

"The bass know the tide will be carrying dinner their way," Tony told me so many times that I soon became a believer.

Much of what I described earlier about the holding patterns of stripers searching for a meal at various stages of the tide applies equally to fishing with natural baits from bridges, piers, and docks.

The key is presenting the natural bait in much the same manner as the current would normally carry it along. Because of the pressure of the current, it's difficult to fish with natural baits by casting up into the flow of the current. As such, the downcurrent flow is where most bait-fishing devotees present their offering.

Many bridge and dock anglers employ the same bottom rigs they'd normally use from the surf or a boat, as described in other chapters. They are particularly effective when used with crab, clam, squid, and other baits customarily fished on the bottom.

By far the most effective baits are live baits, such as sandworms, eels, herring, menhaden, hickory shad, mackerel, snapper blues, croaker, spot, and other small fish. Keep in mind that stripers will eat practically any small fish. Years ago it was common practice to use small winter flounder as bait, and blackfish were popular, too. Today those species, and many others, are covered by state regulations. Exercise care not to violate the law by using fish that are protected by regulations.

When using live baits it's wise to use a 20- or 30-pound-test fluorocarbon leader. Often a striper will ingest the bait, and the heavier leader will prevent the chafing that could occur in the event you tied your hook directly to the end of your light line.

Double a couple of feet of the terminal end of your line using a surgeon's loop, and then tie 3 or 4 feet of fluorocarbon leader to the double line using a surgeon's knot. This makes a nice easy-to-tie, smooth connection, with no need to use a swivel.

When I'm using one or two sandworms as bait I'll snell a 2/0 or 3/0 Claw-style hook with a baitholder shank directly to the end of the leader. While holding the sandworm securely, wait for it to open its mouth, then slide the hook into it and thread the worm onto the hook, exiting ½ inch or so from the head. Then thread on a second sandworm. Both will be held securely in place with the barbs of the baitholder shank.

If the tidal flow is moderate, you need only drift the sea worms out with the current, where they'll slip and slide, with the rips and eddies moving them about where a hungry striper will quickly find them. If the current is strong, and you want to get the baits down a bit deeper, just add a small rubber-cored sinker to the leader a couple of feet ahead of the bait.

Tony the fireman would walk back and forth for hours from bridges spanning coastal rivers. When a striper grabbed the sandworms, it was an instant hookup. He'd call, "Coming through," as he worked his way toward shore to beach the bass while other anglers cleared their lines.

Really exciting fishing can be enjoyed while using live baitfish. Rig up with the same leader, but use a Claw-, Beak-, or Live Bait style hook in sizes 4/0 through 6/0. You can use live herring, mackerel, spot or croaker, or many other small fish, and especially eels.

The key in presenting the live bait is hooking it so it can swim effortlessly in the current and does not spin. With eels, run the hook in the lower lip or out the upper lip. Some anglers run the hook through the eye sockets, which is also effective.

When using spot, croaker, herring, or menhaden, run the hook through the fleshy part of the back just forward of the dorsal fin. Hooked in this manner, the fish can swim effortlessly and will remain alive and active for a long period of time. You can also hook smaller baits through the lips.

As with the sandworm baits, just ease the baitfish out in the current and permit it to swim about in the rips and eddies formed as the water flows beneath the dock, pier, or bridge. A lively baitfish won't hesitate to move about a lot, and many anglers simply pay out line: The more area the baitfish covers, the greater the opportunity of a hungry striper spotting it.

Often you can feel excited activity as a baitfish is being stalked and hurriedly swims about, attempting to seek freedom from the stalker. Often the hookup comes in a flash. A good approach is to permit the striper to move off with the bait, pointing the rod in the direction the line is moving, then locking the reel in gear and lifting back smartly to set the hook. Then it's just a matter of holding on!

Fishing with a breeches buoy rig is still another effective technique to use while fishing with live baitfish from bridges, docks, and piers. The technique is covered in detail in other chapters, and enables you to precisely present live bait from the structure from which you're fishing.

Fishing from bridges, piers, and docks is a challenge, make no mistake. It takes dedication to study the body of water surrounding each structure, knowing the relationship of tides to the movement of stripers and the forage they are regularly seeking. The rewards, once you master the basics, can be extremely pleasant, particularly when the tide is right and the stripers are lined up along the shadow line, waiting for a meal to be swept their way.

CHAPTER 6

Bass on a Fly Cast

It has often been said that fly fishing is one of the most graceful art forms. I totally agree with that assessment. It's a kind of fishing that grows on you. In the beginning a caster may appear to be most ungraceful; with patience and practice, however, the timing of a ballerina develops, and a tuft of feathers and bucktail is delivered with accuracy and grace.

Fly fishing is unlike other forms of casting. With a spinning or multiplying outfit the lure is cast and the lure's weight carries it to the target, with the line trailing. In fly fishing the fly is almost weightless. The weight to cast the fly is instead built into the fly line, and it's the fly line that's cast; its tapered leader turns over and becomes an extension of the fly line, in turn presenting the fly.

The last decade has seen the greatest growth in saltwater fly fishing in history. In great part the striped bass has contributed to this growth, for this sterling, unpredictable saltwater game fish has drawn many freshwater anglers to worship at its shrine, having first experienced fly fishing on a swift-running river for trout or lily-pad-pocked pond for bass. Even for veteran striper anglers, the challenge of catching a linesider on the long rod has roped many in.

I had my beginnings in saltwater fly fishing in the Florida Keys, where I got to meet and fish with many truly expert fly casters, many of whom tutored me in the skills of the long rod, most notably Lefty Kreh. In one easy lesson he taught me to double haul,

Left: John Creenan hooked this school striper while casting a Clouser salt water minnow fly in the tide rips off the Rockaways on Long Island while using an 8-weight outfit.

and immediately I extended my casts with ease by a full 50 percent. Stu Apte preached his relaxing style and taught me that timing and execution were the keys, and soon I relaxed and stopped trying to "push" the casts.

My first striper on a fly rod was landed from the marsh banks on the south shore of the Manasquan River, where the Crystal Point Marina now stands. It was a school striper of 7 pounds and struck a white marabou streamer. Talk about an adrenaline rush. When I hooked that bass, I was electrified like never before!

It was in 1965 or thereabouts that a group of us began what at the time was called the Salt Water Fly Rodders of America. A driving force behind the organization was Fred Schrier, who at the time worked for *Salt Water Sportsman* magazine. Fred began a New Jersey chapter. Luminaries such as Joe Brooks, Lefty Kreh, Hollie Hollenbeck, and Stu Apte headed north to Jersey each spring. There they joined with Jersey long-rod devotees Mark Sosin, Cap Colvin, George Cornish, Dick Wood, and others to fish the waters of Barnegat Bay each spring when the stripers arrived. We caught many school stripers and early-arriving bluefish, but also learned much from the veterans.

Since those early days saltwater fly-fishing equipment has enjoyed a development that has aided both veteran anglers and newcomers. Featherweight graphite and graphite composite rods that have a power delivery have replaced the heavy fiberglass rods and the soft actions of the past. The knuckle-buster single-action fly reels with their ratchety drag systems gave way to beautiful machined reels with drags as smooth as silk. And the evolution of the modern fly line, thanks to pioneers like Leon Martuch of Scientific Anglers, was perhaps the single most dynamic development to propel saltwater fly fishing to where it is today.

FLY-FISHING TACKLE

Basic saltwater fly-fishing equipment, consisting of a rod, reel, and line, is classified using a numeric system. The range for general saltwater fishing is from the lightest, a 5-weight outfit, to the heaviest, a 14-weight. For striped bass fishing the standard for many years was a 10-weight outfit. Over time many of us have come to realize that a 10-weight or heavier is really overkill unless you're specifically targeting very large stripers.

The norm, and one I would recommend for newcomer or veteran, is an 8- or 9-weight outfit. A perfectly balanced outfit of this weight, with the reel loaded with 200 yards of 20-pound-test backing and 100 feet of fly line, gives you 700 feet of line and a powerful rod and reel that will enable you to land very large stripers. Patience and knowing your equipment are the keys.

Fly line for saltwater fly fishing for stripers includes four basic types: floating, slow-sinking, moderate-sinking, and fast-sinking lines. You should choose a line suited to the type of fishing you'll be doing: from a floating line while fishing shallow flats in bays and rivers, on up to a fast-sinking line when probing deep-water haunts of stripers.

The Quad Tip system of interchangeable tip line has grown in popularity in recent years. It offers line tips with attached loops for easy changing, a small-diameter running line, and an extra-stiff braided monofilament core to help cast big saltwater flies during the windy conditions you'll often encounter.

Throughout this book I've noted that for every striper you see chasing bait on the surface, there may be hundreds in the depths. Recognizing that stripers often feed deep, many fly casters employ sinking-tip lines in a variety of weights, all designed to get the line deep. The tips range in weight from 175 to 575 grains, and have sink rates from 4 to 8 inches per second, which quickly gets them down into the depths at which the stripers often feed.

The leader also plays an important role in that it becomes an extension of the fly line, and turning the fly over so that line and leader rest perfectly straight at the conclusion of the cast. The tip of most fly lines approximates the diameter of 30-pound-test line, and is looped onto a leader with a butt section of 20- or 30-pound test fluorocarbon, which in turn is tapered down to 16- or 12-pound test.

In southern climes fly fishermen often use leaders measuring 12 feet in overall length. When seeking striped bass, however, I've found an 8-foot leader more than adequate, and often fish with a leader measuring just 6 feet in length. The conditions encountered when striper fishing often entail minimal false casting, with but a single false cast or double haul before shooting the fly to the target. I find this more easily accomplished with a shorter leader.

Here, too, the refractive index of fluorocarbon leader material makes it virtually invisible in the water, and when looped to a fly line designed expressly for striped bass results in a perfect combination that will bring you strikes from the wariest striper. Make certain to use 100 percent fluorocarbon for the ultimate in knot strength, low abrasion, and virtual invisibility in the water. Use a blood knot to tie a new tippet section of the same diameter to the tip of your leader, as the tippet length of a tapered leader decreases each time you cut off and retie a fly.

FLIES FOR BASS

The creations of fly tiers never cease to amaze me. When I began fly fishing for stripers there was a relative handful of patterns. Today there are thousands, many painstakingly tied to imitate sand eels, spearing, baby bunker, big bunker, mullet, squid, herring, crabs, and every other type of forage on which stripers feed. I doubt if there's a single fly that hasn't at one time or another brought a strike from a hungry striper. The majority of striper flies are tied on size 2 through 3/0 stainless-steel O'Shaughnessy-style hooks, although some patterns extend the range of sizes.

The proliferation of fly patterns does have a drawback, however. I've seen many anglers become so engrossed in fly patterns

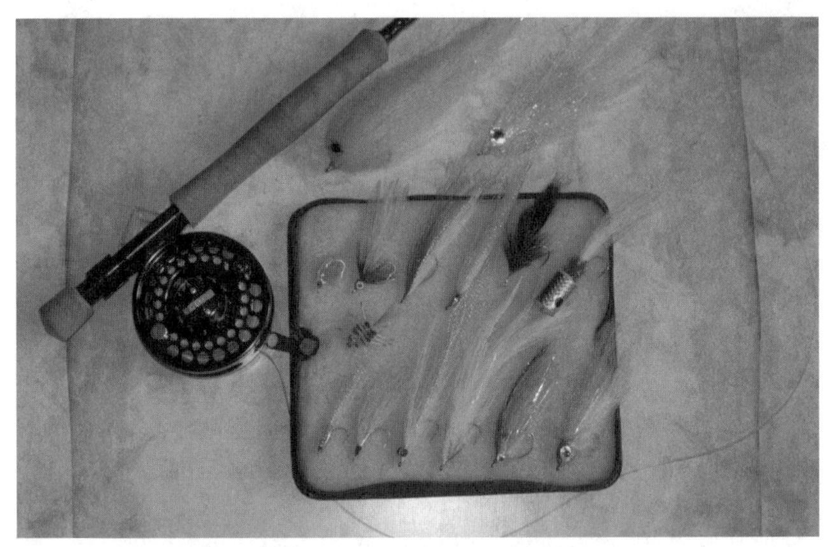

Well-known fly tier Bob Popovics tied this selection of 15 saltwater flies, all of which will produce stripers. They key is using a fly that comes close in size, shape, and color to the natural forage on which the stripers are feeding.

and attempting to "match the hatch"—to use the parlance of freshwater anglers—that they spend an inordinate amount of time constantly trying new patterns and changing flies, as opposed to fishing with a proven pattern. My fly box admittedly doesn't compare with those of many long-rod devotees. Indeed, I can honestly say that I'll often fish with but one pattern for weeks or even months at a time, simply because I've built up confidence in it, have mastered its use, and have enjoyed the rewarding strikes it has brought me.

This is not to imply that you should use but a single pattern. A good approach would be one that I used when I wrote *The Complete Book of Saltwater Fishing*. I asked well-known fly tier and innovator Bob Popovics of Seaside Park, New Jersey, to tie me a selection of 15 flies that he felt would suit any situation along the seacoast. Within that selection would be flies to accommodate everything from the most cautious to the least cautious fish in the sea. His selection, a photo of which is included herein, is equally applicable when seeking striped bass in particular. The flies represent a wide range of natural forage species, ranging from large bunker to a tiny crab, all of which are part of a striper's diet at one time or another.

While each fly pattern has its application, I'd be remiss were I not to identify the saltwater Clouser Minnow developed by noted fly tier Bob Clouser as my favorite for all-around effectiveness when seeking striped bass. I prefer the epoxy-head model with beaded eyes, as it'll withstand the ravages of the occasional bluefish attack. Among my favorite color patterns are the brown and white with gold Mylar, which is especially effective when striped bass are feeding on sand eels, sand bugs, and small crabs. The chartreuse and white with silver Mylar is another fine color, especially when spearing, rainfish, anchovies, and the fry of other species are plentiful and being fed on by linesiders. Blue and white with silver Mylar is still another effective color when mullet, herring, and mackerel are the target. There are, however, Clousers tied in every color of the rainbow, and I suspect they'll all bring strikes when worked through the water table where the bass are searching for a meal. I've watched a Clouser retrieved through a school of baitfish, and suspect it's those typical big, beady eyes and tantalizing bucktail and Mylar, which so resembles the typical baitfish, that excites bass into striking.

FLY-FISHING TECHNIQUES

Both boat- and beach-based anglers enjoy fly fishing for stripers. Much as when employing other types of tackle, you've got to know the water, know the limitations of your tackle, and, where appropriate, make adjustments.

Perhaps the quickest way to build up confidence with the fly rod is to take the time to master fly casting first. Toward this end, the best approach is to seek out a pond or low-to-the-water dock and develop your casting skills. Practicing on the water enables you to get the feel of the fly line, executing a roll cast, lifting the line smartly from the water, false casting, and eventually executing the double haul so you can lay out a reasonable length of fly line with ease.

The single most important advice I can offer is not to concern yourself with distance. In the vast majority of casting situations, whether from boat or beach, distance is not the major consideration—accuracy is. By far most stripers that I've landed have been with casts of 50 to 75 feet. Casting distances such as this are relatively easy to master thanks to today's excellent tackle. Just practice and be comfortable with casts of this distance, and leave the 100-footers to those who feel they're important, which is seldom the case in targeting stripers.

The easiest way to become a believer is to participate in a feeding frenzy of stripers. For boat fishermen this kind of situation presents itself most often during the fall, when huge schools of menhaden, mullet, spearing, rainfish, and other forage begin to vacate bay and river waters as the water temperature drops. It's at this time that stripers are feeding in anticipation of the long winter. They're often reckless, and work in wolf packs that attack the helpless forage from below, while terns and gulls attack the same forage from the sky.

It's an exciting moment to depart a coastal inlet and, as you cruise along the beach, see the sky alive with birds, while feeding stripers churn the water to a maelstrom of activity. I've experienced this off the Saco River in Maine, off Chatham on Cape Cod, and on Montauk, Sandy Hook, and the Outer Banks of Hatteras. It's a predictable fall occurrence, one of the few predictable events when seeking "the prince of the unpredictables."

The key in a situation such as this is to position your boat to take advantage of wind and current to carry you to the fish, as opposed to racing up and perhaps spooking them. Then it becomes simply a matter of positioning yourself in a clear spot on board—the bow or stern, away from antennas, rod racks, outriggers, hard tops, or other obstructions—and executing your casts to the feeding fish.

Always keep in mind there are many more fish in the depths than you see chasing bait on top. Many newcomers to fly fishing are so excited to hook up that when their fly enters the water, they immediately begin to retrieve. Often it's better to hesitate; by knowing the sink rate of your line, you can determine just how deep it's settled before beginning your retrieve, which will often result in more strikes than an immediate retrieve.

You can also approach the fish from downcurrent or downwind and stem the tide, casting to the fish as they chase bait. This is most easily accomplished when you've a skilled crew and helmsman, although it can be difficult casting into the wind if it's strong.

Nothing builds up your confidence level with respect to casting, delivering, and retrieving the fly, hooking the striper, and bringing it to boatside like a blitz such as the one just described. In no time you learn how to deliver the fly quickly and accurately, keep the line taut as you retrieve, set the hook, and play and land the fish.

Jim Carey holds the flats boat in place with his push pole while Bob Katsara plays a striper on a fly rod. The bass was hooked while sight casting along the shallows of the North Shore while sailing from Montauk Harbor, New York.

For newcomers in particular I'd recommend that you begin fly fishing by enlisting the services of a professional fly-fishing guide. There are many fine guides along the coast who specialize in this fishing. They have flats-style boats built expressly for fly fishing, unencumbered with the extraneous hardware found on stock boats, which can cause grief if you're trying to hold your footing on an often choppy ocean with loose fly line resting at your feet.

Sight Casting

While the excitement of feeding bass and a sky alive with gulls is thought of as the ultimate in fly rodding for stripers, there's a type of fishing that is difficult to beat, and that's sight casting to individual fish. It is the nearest thing to bonefishing on the flats you'll ever experience, and some of us believe it's often more difficult making a presentation.

Sight fishing is most often practiced in the shallow flats along a protected shoreline—not the open surf—where an angler is positioned in the bow and poled across 3- to 4-foot-deep water. I've done this off the North Shore of Montauk, in the quiet reaches of Barnegat Bay in Jersey, and in dozens of coves, creeks, and tributaries of the Chesapeake Bay and numerous other striper locales.

The striped bass move as singles, two or three fish at a time, or even in schools of a dozen or more fish. They're usually spotted as they move along the shallows—that thin line that exists along most beaches where there's clean sand bottom, broken by patches

Fly fishermen often pole across shallow flats near shore where they sight cast to stripers cruising along the shoreline searching for a meal. The bass are often moving quite fast, from single fish, to pods of half a dozen fish, and occasionally an entire school. The key is in the presentation, which must be made quickly, with minimal false casting, and placing the fly within the sight range of the moving fish.

of rock or grass beds. As the fish move through, searching for a meal, they're upon you in a flash.

Fast-moving individual stripers require a much quicker presentation even than bonefish, which can often be spotted at a great distance methodically cruising along a flat. With stripers you've often got to roll cast, lift the line into the air, and shoot it to the target all in one quickly executed motion.

In thin water—where it's best to use either a floating or slow-sinking line—you should time your retrieve based on where the fly has dropped in and the direction in which the fish is moving. As soon as the fish is within 5 feet or so of the fly, begin your retrieve. Here it's important that you point the rod in the direction of the line, and begin your stripping retrieve so that the fly moves ahead enticingly and steadily, without any slack in the line. This is when you've got to be alert to wind and current—a belly in the line just won't cut it. If you time everything perfectly, the striper will spot the fly, accelerate toward it, gills spread, inhale the fly, close down on it, and turn, at which time you should lift back smartly to set the hook, and hold on!

While poling along the flats, use polarized sunglasses and pay special attention to the patches of open sand bottom, for it is here that you're apt to most easily spot the moving fish. When they're over rock or grass they're tough to see. Don't fiddle with false casts to extend a lot of line. Get the fly in the air and shoot it to your target.

As you're poling along the shoreline and adjacent flats, you'll often come to points of land, no matter whether you're fishing a broad expanse of sound, bay, river, or creek waters. On a moving tide, stripers will often take up residence on the downcurrent side of the point; this is where a back eddy often forms and forage such as grass shrimp, crabs, and baitfish congregate. It's also a spot where a bass can stay out of the main current where it has to expend energy. Approach the point from offshore, and cast cross-current to the moving flow, permitting the current to carry your fly much like a baitfish struggling in the current. Work your fly from right on the shoreline into the deep, and through the eddy formed by the point of land. Often you'll be rewarded with a smorgasbord, as stripers, blues, and weaks will congregate in such spots waiting for an easy meal to be swept their way.

It's not unusual to find many points of land as you pole along, some extending just 20 feet or so from shore. Some are sandy points, other rocky promontories, while others are lined with marsh grass. Give several casts to each, and you'll be regularly rewarded. Often when two of us are casting to such a spot, one angler will fish with a sinking fly such as a Lefty's Deceiver, Clouser, or Half-and-Half, while I'll use a topwater slider or a popping bug. The topwater lure will often act as an attractor, quickly bringing up a fish to investigate on your very first cast. Sometimes they're just lookers, but many will boil on the topwater fly like it was the last food in the bay.

Bridges and Jetties

Bridges also offer many fly-casting opportunities. I've enjoyed excellent night fly fishing at the Chesapeake Bay Bridge and Tunnel complex at Virginia Beach. The lights of the bridge illuminate the water for miles and establish the longest shadow line I've ever fished. At times you can stem the tide and see a dozen or more stripers, all with their noses tight to the shadow line, waiting for an unsuspecting crab, shrimp, or small fish to be carried to them. Then they dart out, engulf it, and promptly return to the shadow line to wait for seconds.

Depending on the flow of the current, you can stem the tide while positioned in the shadows beneath the bridge and execute your cast up and into the current, stripping it back toward the shadow line as you retrieve. At other times you can position the bow of your boat directly on the shadow line and cast up and across current at a 45-degree angle, permitting the current to carry the fly toward the fish as you strip your retrieve.

There are also times when forage species such as menhaden and spearing congregate in tight packs of hundreds of fish, especially at slack tide, milling about in the lights. It's then—especially when there's no current along the shadow line—that the bass move away from the shadow line and unmercifully attack them. Then it's just a matter of positioning your boat and executing casts into the feeding fish.

Another spot available to the long-rod gentry who fish from boats is wherever groins, jetties, natural rocky promontories, or breakwaters extend seaward. Striped bass often take up residence among the rocks along the ends of these structures. They know that many baitfish schools travel parallel to the beaches, and must move around the fronts of these structures to pass them.

Positioning your boat offshore of such spots and casting in among the waves crashing on the rocks can often result in exciting sport. It's always important to keep someone alert at the helm, so the incoming waves don't push you too close to the structure. Once a fish is hooked, keep your rod tip high in the air and exercise maximum control of the fish so it doesn't get back into the rocks.

Blind casting is another very effective method of catching stripers, especially where bay and river waters are relatively shallow. At the birthplace of the Salt Water Fly Rodders of America in Barnegat Bay, New Jersey, the majority of the casting was done blind, in water ranging from 3 to 6 feet deep, using sinking lines that got down near the bottom, where the stripers were usually feeding on spearing and grass shrimp.

I'll often drift across a particularly good area using either a spinning or popping outfit and probe it using plugs or leadhead jigs and bait tails, often with a teaser ahead of the primary lure. If I begin to score, it tells me stripers are in the area. Then I'll switch over to fly fishing.

Fishing from jetties is extremely difficult for the fly caster. You've got to worry about keeping the fly line in a stripping basket so it doesn't get fouled in the rocks, you're usually confronted with wind, and then there are the waves crashing around you. On some groins and jetties you can manage, but always wear Korkers on your boots or waders to secure your footing.

The key for those occasions when conditions permit you to fish from the rocks is to concentrate on lots of short casts, working the fly along the jetty rocks at an angle from where you're standing. An ideal situation is when it's calm with an offshore wind, and the bait congregates in the corner, or the pocket, where the rocks meet the beach. Often you can stand there and shoot casts up along the beach, working them back toward the rocks. Here strikes often come just as you're about to lift the fly from the water to execute another cast. Do the same thing while fishing the beaches as well.

Fly Fishing the Surf

Fishing from the beach with a fly rod isn't that much different from doing so with spinning or multiplying tackle. Admittedly, it's a bit more difficult, simply because you've usually got to wear a stripping basket to keep your fly line from constantly becoming tangled about your legs, especially along surf where there's constant wave action.

At many of the spots I've fished from a boat while sight casting; as I described earlier, I've also fished from the beach and while wading. Usually being low to the water while wading prevented me from sight casting, as I didn't have the vantage offered while standing on the casting bow of a boat. Instead, I just walked along, blind casting. I've enjoyed excellent results while walking up several feet from the water, blind casting over rocks and grass beds. As I strip the fly, I keep my rod tip low to the water and pointed in line with the fly line, to keep the line taut. I literally strip the fly right up onto the sand, and many strikes are received just a rod's length from the tip as a stripers home in to engulf it before it reaches the sanctuary of the thin water along the beach.

Along the surf I'm especially aware of how close the fish often feed to the beach. On all three of the surf beach formations you're apt to encounter—gently sloping, deep drop-off, or with sloughs inside a bar formation—stripers will often feed less than 20 feet from the sand. The churning action of the waves exposes sand bugs, crabs, and sand eels; other forage species also seek the thin water, which ranges from inches to a couple of feet deep.

The ideal situation for fishing the surf is an offshore wind. This makes executing your casts relatively easy, especially when coupled with calm surf. When you get this kind of surf, coupled with baitfish such as spearing or sand eels late in the fall, it's especially exciting to fish the surf at night. Often in the millpond quiet of the surf caused by the offshore wind—usually northwest—the baitfish will get tight to the beach, and you can not only see the bait nervously swimming about but also see the stripers charging into it with a vengeance.

There are times when surf conditions are prohibitively wild. This is especially true when you've a strong onshore wind, such as those nasty winds from the northeast, and the surf is high, breaking on the offshore bars or rolling wildly onto the beach. Still, stripers often feed in water that makes you ponder how they can even swim in it, let alone feed. While it is extremely difficult to cast in such a wind, let alone strip a fly properly, sometimes just getting the fly 30

Fly casting for stripers while wading shallow bays and rivers produces exciting sport. The stripping basket is used to keep the fly line from dragging in the water while executing a cast.

or 40 feet off the beach will bring quick strikes. Here again, it's a matter of making a roll cast, and then shooting the line quickly, and quickly gaining control so the line is taut and you're able to strip the fly without a belly in the line. Believe me, when a striper takes hold in that kind of surf you're in for the fight of a lifetime.

Toward that end, it's important to always be patient, regardless of where you hook a fish with fly tackle. When a reel is screaming

The author was among a group of fly casters who established the Salt Water Fly Rodders of America in 1965, when saltwater fly fishing was in its infancy. He still loves to use the long rod from beach and boat, and hooked this beauty from the New Jersey surf.

and line pouring off, some anglers panic. Just take your time. You have fully 700 feet of fly line and backing, and even the biggest striper is going to run out of steam before it spools you. As soon as the fish slows, especially when fishing the surf, apply pressure with the rod held high, and often the seas will help you turn it around. Take care to follow the fish, for often it won't just head out to sea but will move up and down the beach instead. I've sometimes had to run at a quick pace to just keep up with a wild striper that never moved more than 100 feet from the sand, but peeled off 150 yards of line in short order as it went up the beach with a swift current from the south. Turns out that most of the wild fish are those 15- to 20-pounders that had their vitamins.

You'd do well to rise early to consistently take stripers from the beach. I like to be on the sand a good hour before first light, as often the fish will be especially active at that time. You'll see bait herded tight to the beach and nervous, knowing that the heavyweights are waiting to charge in toward the sand to engulf them. There are mornings when you'll draw a blank, but often you'll get up to a couple of hours of good action—and then, just as the sun sticks its head above the horizon, the stripers will turn off and the bait will settle down. This is not only a fall pattern, but especially true among fish that reside along the surf during the warm summer months.

If you just like walking and casting, by all means don't hesitate to put on a bathing suit and fish the same beaches that are filled with sunbathers and tourists during the summer months anywhere along the Northeast coast. The surf is often warm and the weather pleasant as the sun goes down; during the summer months in particular, the stripers will move in from offshore to cruise along the surf line and feed upon whatever happens by. I should note that while the princely striper may be your target, often you'll be rewarded with strikes from many other exciting species, including weakfish, bluefish, fluke, Spanish mackerel, little tunny, hickory shad, and herring, all of which will give you and your tackle a workout.

I've often walked for hours, casting and retrieving with fly tackle, and just when I thought all was hopeless I've seen the line come tight as a hungry bass takes the fly. It's what fly fishing is all about—patience and perseverance, knowing your tackle, and having confidence in that fly tied to the end of your leader.

CAPTAIN TONY
YAMAHA

CHAPTER 7

Chumming for Bass

Chumming can be easily defined as "dropping pieces of food into the water to attract fish to a baited hook." It can be done from a boat or shore. It relies on giving the fish two options: either expending energy foraging for a meal over a wide area, or simply moving toward the source of food that is being carried along by the current. Invariably the latter option is chosen, as it's the easiest way for a hungry fish to fill its stomach. Striped bass are no exception, hence the popularity of chumming.

There is, however, a lot more to chumming than just dropping food into the water. Only after you've observed a veteran angler methodically chumming and catching stripers, while others seemingly employing the same technique fail to draw so much as a strike, can you appreciate the science this method entails.

Chumming for stripers is not something new to the fraternity who seek this princely game fish. It dates back to 1890, or perhaps earlier, when bassing clubs were in vogue among men of means. Many clubs owned choice waterfront property throughout Massachusetts and the Elizabethan Islands in particular, where the art of chumming was practiced. Indeed, elaborate stands were built, with strong supporting members placed into holes that were first drilled into natural rock promontories extending seaward. In turn wooden planking was placed in what at best could be described as an irregular pattern, to provide both chummer and angler with adequate footing.

Left: Captain Tony DeLernia just netted this striper for noted outdoor writer Gary Caputi, who hooked it while chumming in the East River off Manhattan.

The clubs were most notable on Martha's Vineyard, the Pasque Islands, and Cuttyhunk, although they sprang up wherever the location lent itself to accessing water frequented by the sought-after striped bass.

Researching records of these clubs leads to a conclusion that was appropriate more than a century ago—and just as valid today: When stripers are hungry, they'll respond to almost any food that is presented to them. The men who chummed in that early era of sportfishing employed just about anything a fish could eat, including herring, mackerel, and menhaden—all fish that were easily obtained, oily, and, when ground, provided a chum that readily attracted linesiders. Chummers would sometimes row out and liberally chum an area just off the stands that extended seaward, while others dispensed the ground-up concoction from the stands. The stripers came to know a free meal was in the offing, and responded in kind, much to the delight of the casters using vintage tackle.

Chunks of common eel, sand lance, and other small baitfish also proved an attractor, as did crushed crabs and, would you believe, lobster! Yes, it was not unusual for chummers to crush lobsters and dispense the delicacy into the sea, while casters baited up with a chunk of the meaty lobster tail. In that era lobsters were plentiful among the rocky outcroppings, and stripers never hesitated to enjoy a meal should one of the macrurous crustaceans venture from its rocky lair.

Chumming from the bass stands of that era was admittedly for the aristocrat, who was assisted by a chummer and often a gaffer, who would position himself to plant a gaff into a heavy striper and help get it to shore. These anglers used bamboo cane rods, some even split bamboo in its infancy; knucklebuster reels with no internal drag, other than a leather drag affixed to the crossbars of the reel; and 9- or 12-thread Cuttyhunk Irish linen line. It must have been exciting fishing, not unlike today's jetty fishing, where precarious footing, rough seas, and crashing windswept waves provide a challenge second to none. Those who share my opinion of jetty fishing for stripers—as the most challenging kind of all—know I would have been right at home casting bait to stripers drawn within range by a trusty chummer.

My first experience at chumming for stripers didn't occur until the 1940s, when my dad and I repaired to Rock Hall, Maryland, hard on the shores of the broad expanse of the Chesapeake Bay. We boarded a charter boat whose captain joined a fleet of half a dozen other charter rigs all anchored side by side, with several of the boats tied together so they wouldn't swing in the current. The small fleet positioned itself daily along the edge of a drop-off, where currents carried the chum along a rip line and stripers moved up to enjoy the free lunch.

The school stripers, ranging from 3 to 5 pounds, moved into the chum line of tiny grass shrimp; at times every boat was hooked up. An occasional white perch spiced the action. What seemed like an endless school of "rock," as striped bass are called in the Chesapeake, provided arm-tiring action with the light outfits. Then, just as the current slowed and the rip line disappeared, the action stopped, almost as if you'd thrown a switch.

The bass were well aware that the current regularly carried food, so they'd taken up station along the edge of the rip, where shrimp, crabs, small fish, and other forage would be plentiful. That same current carried our shrimp chum, but when the current slowed at the approach of slack tide, even the chum settled to the bottom. It was a lesson in timing, knowing where to be at a particular stage of the tide, and then how to use the chum effectively.

Therein lies the secret to successful chumming, whether from boat or shore. You can't just arbitrarily position yourself, begin chumming, and expect to catch striped bass. Boat anglers have a wide array of nautical charts available to them, which when care-

Vin Sparano excels at chumming with grass shrimp. The key is to dispense just a few shrimp at a time, permitting them to be carried along with the current. Bait with four or five of the tiny shrimp and drift them back in the chum line for exciting action.

fully analyzed offer insights as to just where striped bass congregate to feed. Then it simply becomes a matter of positioning the boat so that chum is carried via the current to where the linesiders have taken up station.

Many examples come to mind. Glancing at a nautical chart of the northern New Jersey coastline immediately shows several choice locales. The Shrewsbury Rocks extend from shore to a buoy that marks the seaward perimeter. The massive natural rock formation strewn across the bottom shows up on a fishfinder as peaks and valleys. There are mussel beds clinging to the rocks, an abundance of crabs and lobsters, along with cunner, sea bass, and tautog, all of which are forage for stripers. Schools of sand eels often invade the area, which is surrounded by miles of flat, sand bottom, none of which is conducive to holding bait or fish. By anchoring and dispensing chum so it is carried across the rocks by the current, you have an excellent opportunity to score.

The Sandy Hook peninsula also offers many fine chumming locales. Most notable is Flynn's Knoll, a patch of high bottom surrounded by deep-water shipping channels where stripers and bait tend to congregate. Another spot is Romer Shoals, whose lighthouse and adjoining flats are a gathering spot for not only striped bass, but bluefish and weakfish, too, and it's not uncommon to have all three species invade your chum line.

On an ebbing tide, the current extending from the point of the Hook in a southeasterly direction is very swift, forming a rip line where the deep-water channel clashes with the flats to the south. Here, too, the bass will take up station on the ebb to feed on the huge quantities of food being carried seaward from Sandy Hook and Raritan Bays. The same spot is completely void of a rip or fish on the flooding tide, highlighting the importance of timing.

On the Sandy Hook Bay side of the peninsula there are chumming opportunities galore. The shallows of Horseshoe Cove regularly attract huge schools of spearing, menhaden, and other forage, and stripers regularly visit the area in their never-ending quest for a meal.

In the open bay there is the Earle Naval Ammunition Pier, which extends well out into the bay, creating rips and currents where bait is carried along with the normal flow of the tide.

Moving up into the Shrewsbury River, the bridge joining Highlands with the Sandy Hook peninsula is another haven for stripers intent on letting the current bring a meal to them. It's a natural for a boatman who wants to lure them to his chum line. The stripers often take up station before the bridge abutments, facing into the tidal flow, where a dead spot develops as the current flows around the abutment. By anchoring up from the icebreakers or abutments and permitting the chum to be carried to the bridge, you're certain to draw stripers to your hook baits.

The nautical charts of the northern New Jersey coast are used here as an example. Charts of Montauk, Long Island, or Buzzards Bay, Massachusetts, or the Chesapeake Bay Bridge and Tunnel complex, or the broad expanse of San Francisco Bay will all provide similar insights into where you should set up your chum line. The same holds true for the myriad charts of every bay, river, and estuary along the coast.

The size of the boat you use for chumming isn't important. I've caught stripers on everything from oar-powered rowboats up to our 43-foot Post, the *Linda June*. There is, however, the safety factor, which should never be overlooked in any kind of fishing. Make certain you've a seaworthy hull before venturing forth, especially into the broad expanse of ocean or sound waters that can become nasty in a matter of minutes.

SELECTING CHUM

Chumming for striped bass is perhaps more popular today than at any time in the last century. The forage that can be used as chum includes most of the food found in the water frequented by the princely striper. Determining what to use as chum is a matter of personal choice, but there are some guidelines that can be followed.

Use a chum that consists of forage indigenous to the area, and that bass are accustomed to feeding on. In protected bays and rivers the grass shrimp constitutes a major portion of the striper's diet, hence its popularity as chum. Ground menhaden, when dispensed with chunks of menhaden, also makes a potent chum, as does herring or mackerel. In recent years the sea clam industry began providing fishermen with a by-product that would normally go to waste—the soft clam bellies that remained after the choice firm clam meat was removed for chowder and clam fritters. Frozen clam bellies are now used along the entire coast as primary chum, while anglers bait with chunks of the firm clam meat or ribbons of muscle tissue.

Stripers also feed extensively on crabs, primarily blue crabs, but calico and sand crabs as well. Many anglers use the discarded swim fins and insides of cleaned crabs as chum. These are dispensed overboard as a cloudy mass of tiny pieces. Anglers then drift back either small crabs or (preferably) shedder crabs into the chum line, resulting in good scores, especially from bay and river waters.

I still vividly recall the late Captain Otto Reut of the charter boat *First Timer* using sandworms and bloodworms as chum. These squiggly sea worms have always been costly, but Otto always had a couple of hundred aboard, and would cut the worms into five or six pieces and then toss them overboard. Occasionally he'd obtain tapeworms, which are a slimy worm to handle, but apparently a treat for hungry stripers.

His anglers would then drift out a single sandworm threaded on a 1/0 Claw-style hook with a baitholder shank. The effectiveness of sandworm chum was particularly apparent during the early-spring run, where there were few baitfish in residence and the bass had to rummage along the bottom for a meal. In the clear springtime water the stripers often moved so close to the boat that you could see them picking up the pieces of sandworm as quickly as they were tossed overboard.

Tiny sand bugs, which can easily be dug along the surf and range in size from as small as your pinkie nail to a bit larger than a thumbnail, are also a treat for stripers, and a great chum and hook bait. Chunks of squid may also be used. Even black mussels are effective: Crush their paper-thin shells and let the shells and meat be carried with the tide, while baiting with the firm meat of a mussel or two.

Captain Tony DeLernia of Rocket Charters *sails from Manhattan and chums the waters of the East River and lower New York Harbor. The author landed this fat striper while chumming with clam bellies off a power plant near Hells Gate in the East River.*

Always remember that if it's something to eat, and is being carried along by the current, a hungry striper won't pass it up. They're much like us humans: Many are the times when we'll sample something not especially to our liking, but let hunger be the deciding factor.

CHUMMING TOOLS

There are some basic tools you'll need before you set forth. While some chum, such as grass shrimp, is easily dispensed overboard, with other types it's best to use a chum pot of some sort. Many commercially made chum pots are made with ¼- or ½-inch galvanized wire mesh, and are approximately 4 to 5 inches in diameter and 8 to 10 inches deep. They have a lead bottom with a hinged metal top. Chum pots of this type are ideally suited to dispensing ground chum such as clams, menhaden, mackerel, or herring. Most often a frozen chum log is inserted into the chum pot, which is lowered to the bottom via a stout cord. There the chum thaws and oozes from the pot, being carried along the bottom with the current.

If you're using large pieces of chum, especially clam bellies, there aren't many effective chum pots made; the diameter of the mesh is just too small to permit large pieces of clam belly to exit the pot. Many veteran clam belly chummers improvise by using a pull-type crab trap. The pull-type traps are made in two basic models—square and triangular—and made with turkey mesh wire measuring either 1-by-1 inch or 1-by-2 inches in diameter. Two 16-ounce sinkers are wired to the bottom of the pull-trap, which is then filled with clam bellies; snaps are fastened to the hinged doors of the trap to keep them from opening. The trap is then lowered to the bottom, where the current gradually causes the soft clam bellies to be carried from the trap and along the bottom until found by hungry stripers. A hard yank on the trap line periodically helps loosen the thawing clam bellies, and permits them to drift free of the trap.

You'll also need a sharp knife and cutting board. A knife with a serrated blade makes it easier to cut chunks of menhaden, herring, or mackerel as chum. Toward this end, it's a good practice to have all your chum and bait prepared before leaving dockside. Then you can concentrate on both the chumming and fishing once you're anchored up—an important consideration.

In addition to your boat's primary anchor, I strongly recommend a second anchor. Using two anchors is one of the secrets to successful chumming, particularly when fishing open waters, where wind or current are apt to cause your boat to swing excessively. With a pair of anchors you can position your boat so it stays right where you want it, with the chum flowing from the boat and the stripers attracted to it, and in turn to your baited hook. While some may scoff at this suggestion, it must be realized that with 50 or 75 feet of rode your boat can make such wide swings in a strong wind-against-the-current situation that the effectiveness of your chumming effort is completely nullified.

TACKLE

You can effectively chum while using either a popping rod with a multiplying reel, a spinning outfit, or fly-casting tackle. While most striped bass caught chumming are caught on natural baits, there are many occasions when a lure worked through chum slick will bring strikes. For the moment, however, let's concentrate on the tackle that's best suited to using natural baits that complement the chum being used.

Toward this end, I much prefer a multiplying reel to a spinning reel—I feel it gives me better control. This, however, is a matter of personal preference, as both outfits will serve you well when drifting a bait back in the chum line.

You should gear your selection of tackle to the size of the stripers that are generally caught in the area you plan to fish. My observation,

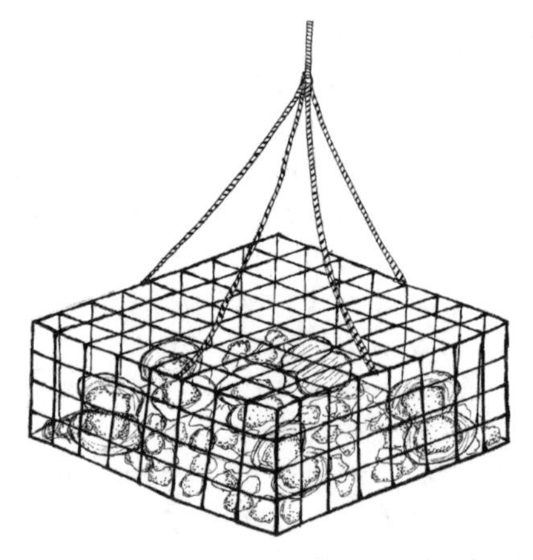

Chumming with clam bellies has become very popular along the entire striper coast. An effective chum dispenser can be made from a crab trap. The trap is filled with frozen clam bellies, weighted with heavy sinkers or a sash weight, tied or clamped shut, and lowered to the bottom beneath an anchored boat. As the clams thaw, the bellies are carried from the trap with the current, attracting stripers to your clam-baited hook.

over many years of fishing on the striper coast, is that 90 percent of the fishermen go forth with tackle far too heavy for the stripers being sought. This is especially true today, for we now have powerful yet lightweight graphite rods, with either multiplying or spinning reels that are equally light in weight, and with line capacities that enable you to spool more than an adequate amount of the new, fine-diameter monofilament, microfilament, or fluorocarbon lines that are available. Considering that when you're chumming you're only using 50 to 75 feet of line for the most part, then if your reel holds 250 yards of line, there's still 675 to 700 feet of line remaining on the reel. When you're dealing with 12- to 15-pound-test line for stripers up to the 20-pound class, or even 20-pound test for heavyweights, that's more than enough line to control the fish. I've seen many anglers using 30- and 50-pound test; this really inhibits their ability to hook fish in the first place, and in conjunction with a heavy rod and reel negates any enjoyment of the fine qualities of catching striped bass.

If I'm using 12- or 15-pound-test line I'll usually employ a surgeon's loop to double the last 18 inches of line. Then I'll use a 3- or 4-foot-long piece of 20-pound-test fluorocarbon leader material, which is tied to the surgeon's loop using a surgeon's knot. It's a nice easy connection to tie, joining the lighter line to the heavier leader. The heavier leader, of nearly invisible fluorocarbon, gives you a measure of insurance; too light a leader will often chafe in the corner of a striper's jaw or become gill-wrapped and break.

There are so many excellent brands of hooks on the market today that almost all of them that are designed as a Live Bait, Claw, or Beak style will work perfectly while chumming. The hook size should be tailored to the size of the bait you plan to use. I'll often use a size 1 or 1/0 Claw style with a baitholder shank when I'm using three or four grass shrimp as bait. If I'm using a chunk of menhaden bait, or a whole clam, then I'll move up to a 4/0 or 5/0 hook of the same style. When chumming I almost always use hooks with a baitholder shank: The barbs in the shank nicely hold the bait in place and prevent it from bunching up on the curve of the hook.

It's also wise to include an assortment of rubber-cored sinkers in your tackle kit. If the current is running swiftly, by adding a little weight you'll get your hook bait down at the same depth at which the chum is traveling.

Sometimes, however, there'll be very little current, and your hook bait may tend to settle too deep while the current is carrying the chum along. Then it's good to employ a Snap Float, a plastic snap-on float, or a Styrofoam popping float with concave head. By positioning the float and using it in conjunction with a small rubber-cored sinker, you can have your bait drifting out at the desired depth.

There are occasions when stripers will hug the depths, especially when they've moved up in a chum line of clam bellies that have settled and drifted along the bottom. Then I'll often use a regular bottom rig, tying a small three-way swivel to the end of my line, tying off a dipsey- or bank-style sinker of sufficient weight to hold bottom to one eye of the swivel, and the leader and hook to the remaining eye. This puts the bait right on the bottom, which is where the chum is, especially if you're using the pull-trap chum dispenser described earlier.

CHUMMING TECHNIQUES

It's important to remember that striped bass vary their feeding habits, depending on conditions. If there are several anglers on board it always pays to begin chumming while alternating the presentation of baits. Fish one bait by livelining it with no weight, have another angler add a rubber-cored sinker to take the bait a bit deeper, put one down on the bottom, and even try a float rig. In this way you've got every level of the water column covered, and will quickly learn just which level the fish are feeding at.

I've often used this approach for a starter, with everyone on board switching over to the successful technique—when suddenly the action stopped. Then it's time to react quickly by going back to the beginning and starting over, for as the current speed or water conditions change the fish may be feeding on chum that is moving at a different depth than was the case earlier.

This is particularly true when you're fishing in water 20 to 30 feet deep. When fishing the 3- to 6-foot shallows of bays and rivers it's not nearly as important, as the stripers will often move throughout the entire water column.

At this point you should be ready to go forth and anchor up at the spot you've chosen for chumming operations. One last task is to check the tide chart. Tide plays a critical role in chumming—perhaps more so than when using other techniques. Many newcomers look for the time of high tide, and on arriving at their location of choice find the tide is still flooding in, whereas they wanted to fish it on the dropping tide. *High tide* refers to the vertical height of the water, and often high tide is reached an hour or more after the water reaches its highest level, after which there is a period of slack water; then the tide begins to ebb and the water level begins to drop.

Take care to study not only the high-tide/low-tide tables, but preferably the slack-water tables for the areas you plan to fish. This will help you get to the fishing grounds of choice and get set up and anchored properly at the optimum time.

I often jot down on the tide charts what my experience has told me the slack period will be. Even then there are times when the slack period may occur earlier, or even later than anticipated as a result of strong wind against or with tidal flow.

Where all of this attention to detail pays off is when you set up at a spot and find it void of fish on a particular stage of tide. You can then look at the tide chart, review the nautical charts, and select a second or even third spot to try. If the bay doesn't produce, then the nearby ocean rips may provide action, or perhaps a visit to a river or bridge abutment where the current will be just perfect.

On approaching a spot where you plan to anchor and chum, it always pays to cruise through the area to determine exactly what the current and wind are doing. Put your boat in neutral and watch how it moves. Then move back up ahead of where you want your boat to be and carefully drop your first anchor. As the boat comes taut on the rode see how it swings in the current and wind, adjusting accordingly as you move up and to the side and drop your second anchor. As the second rode comes taut, you can then compensate by adjusting either one or the other line until you get your boat solidly positioned just where you want it.

Having prepared your chum and rigged all your outfits before arrival, you're ready to commence chumming operations. Now comes the most important decision of the entire outing. A person has to be designated and committed to handling the chumming. This is without question the most critical job on board. All too often it's handled in a haphazard way; as soon as the stripers begin biting, the all-important task of maintaining an unbroken chum line is forgotten, with the fish quickly moving off and not returning.

A method I like to employ aboard the *Linda June* is for each person to handle chumming for an hour at a time. When I have my regular friends on board, we all know the importance of chumming, and switch off regularly, ensuring that this important task is properly handled.

The amount of chum to use, and how often to dispense it overboard, is important. This is a matter of judgment and experience. If you chum too heavily, striped bass will take up station well back in the chum line and gorge on the chum until their stomachs are full. Then they'll just stop feeding, and you won't be able to score.

You want to employ the chum sparingly, so that you attract the striped bass into the chum line, challenging them to pick it up. All the while they'll be moving toward its source, where they'll eventually find your hook bait.

A rule of thumb I've always used is to toss out six to eight pieces of small chum, such as grass shrimp, or three to four pieces of larger chum, such as chunks of bunker, herring, or clam belly. Watch as the current carries it away, and once it's 30 feet or so from the boat, toss out another offering. Toss the pieces at intervals, so they're separated by a few feet. This will often result in the striped bass vying for the pieces as they drift back, and the bass will hurriedly move up the chum line, anxious to get another piece before one of their neighbors does.

With the chum line established, bait up and begin drifting the baits at intervals with one bait on a free line, another with a small sinker, and a third line with a float. The key now becomes keeping the baits drifting at the same speed as the free-drifting pieces of chum. This means applying gentle thumb pressure to the line, so it doesn't overrun, yet is carried effortlessly by the current.

Sometimes I enhance the drift by pulling 12 to 18 inches of line from the reel at a time. Eventually you'll get the technique down pat. Often you'll strip 20 or 25 pulls and suddenly find that all of the strikes are coming at a specific number of pulls of line, which tells you the fish are holding back in the chum line at a specific distance, waiting for the chum—and eventually your hook bait—to be carried to them. This is especially so when the fish are schooled up in a tide rip, or holding in the dead spot just ahead of a bridge abutment or icebreaker.

CHUMMING FROM SHORE

Chumming from shore or structures such as docks, bridges, and piers also can prove effective. Surprisingly, while years ago this technique was held in high esteem by renowned striper anglers, many anglers now prefer just using natural baits or casting artificials. It's admittedly a lot of work to set up a chum line while based on terra firma.

The successful shore-based chummer understands current flow, the timing of tides, and how the flow is affected. When chumming from a bridge, dock, or other structure you'll find that stripers often set up station and feed actively when the current moderates. This is usually an hour before, during, or an hour after the change of high or low tide. These are the times when bass can leisurely move about without struggling in the current.

You can establish a chum line from the same locations you'd normally be fishing with natural baits. This is particularly true when casting from a bridge, dock, or pier. The advantage is that the chum will be carried well beyond where your baits are positioned, with the stripers drawn to the source, where they'll ultimately find your bait. The same chum used by boatmen, be it chunks of anchovy, herring, menhaden, or clam, works equally well. The key is dispensing it into the water where there is sufficient current to establish an effective chum line.

While it can be done, it's admittedly difficult to establish a chum line from a jetty or beach. The key is to determine just how the current is flowing, so that as you drop pieces into the water they are carried away to the same location where you're able to position your bait.

Chumming requires preparation, patience, and continued effort in order to be successful. The rewards can be great, however, for once the stripers move up into the chum line, the fishing is often phenomenal.

Shore-based anglers often chum from bulkheads, docks, and piers. This is the Shinnecock Canal, where as the tide slows an effective chum line of menhaden or butterfish chunks, or clam bellies, can be established from the easily accessible bulkhead.

CHAPTER 8

Trolling

The striped bass troller might well be termed a wanderer. Equipped with a small outboard-powered craft or a spacious sportfisherman, the troller uses his boat to advantage in covering lots of water as he seeks stripers.

At first blush you might think trolling simply a matter of streaming lines astern and cruising along. That notion is quickly dispelled when you observe a veteran troller scoring consistently, while the boats around him fail to draw a strike. As with each of the methods discussed in this book, there's much more to trolling than meets the eye. Through study, application, and perseverance, you too can join that cadre of the successful.

It's not difficult to rig a boat for trolling, and it's important to take the time to do so, as it'll enhance your opportunity to score on the fishing grounds. Because you'll be trolling for what may be hours at a time, rod holders and their proper placement on a boat are important. For most striper trolling applications, I've found that a maximum of three lines works well; put out more and you're inviting tangles. A good combination is to include one rod holder for a line down the middle, placed at the center of the gunwale at the transom. Port and starboard rod holders should also be situated near the stern. Sometimes the rods are placed directly into the rod holders. However, it often is beneficial to use outholders, or rod

Left: Pete Casale holds a big striper hooked by the author on a parachute jig sent into the depths with wire line while trolling off Montauk Point, Long Island.

holders that fit into the mounted rod holder and point out from the side of the boat. When rods are placed in the outholders, it extends the breadth of the boat by the length of the rod used. The rods are parallel with the water and extend out from the side of the boat at a right angle. This keeps the lines well separated. Importantly, the outholders keep the lines low to the water, which permits the lures to work deeper than with the rods placed vertically in the rod holders.

Because you're frequently turning while trolling, it's important that you have safety lines attached to the outholders, using a snap that is in turn attached to the reel. While it seldom happens, outfits have been known to be pulled from the outholder and lost overboard on a tight turn in a rough sea, usually as a result of snagging bottom. The safety line prevents this from happening, and is good insurance.

A good electronic fishfinder is a very useful tool of the troller: It enables you not only to find fish but also to observe the bottom conformation and the depths at which you're trolling. You can then compensate accordingly with respect to the length of line you're trolling, and your speed, both important considerations.

TROLLING TACKLE

Spinning tackle is designed for casting, and really has little application for the troller. I discourage its use, as ultimately it will cause you grief.

Trolling outfits employ multiplying reels, with two general categories most popular. If most of your trolling is done in shallow water, in the protected reaches of bays and rivers, you'll find that a popping rod measuring 6½ feet in overall length and a level-wind casting reel capable of holding a couple of hundred yards of 15- or 20-pound-test line will serve you well.

In open-water fishing, where you're fishing the ocean, sound, or bay in depths of 15 to 60 feet or more, it's important that you select a heavier outfit suited to this type of trolling. Trolling rods that measure 6½ to 7 feet in overall length, rated for 30-pound-test line, with a firm action and slotted butt that fits into the rod holder will serve you well. Trollers who regularly employ large bunker spoons when seeking stripers often use rods measuring up to 9 feet, as this length, when positioned in a outholder, separates the big spoons and helps avoid tangles. In addition, the extra length and soft action of the long tip enhances the action of the spoons and large plugs used with these long rods.

Select a size 3/0 or 4/0 trolling reel with a star drag and capable of holding 250 to 300 yards of 30-pound-test monofilament line. The same-sized reel may be used if you're employing wire line—Monel or stainless steel—as a top shot of 100 yards at the terminal end of the mono, although overall the heavier diameter of wire diminishes the total line capacity of the reel. Many wire-line devotees use Dacron as their backing line, preferring 50-pound test and attaching a 100- to 150-yard length of wire at the terminal end.

Some anglers prefer a level-wind feature on their reel, which lays the line flat on the reel as it is retrieved, avoiding any buildup that may occur if you fail to pay attention while fighting a fish. A line counter is also helpful; this lets you know precisely how much line you have out, an important consideration when you want to fish your lures the exact distance behind the boat where strikes have been received. There may be times when you'll be using wire line, such as Monel or stainless steel, and you'll want a rugged reel.

The broad range of techniques used while trolling for stripers include trolling with monofilament, Dacron, or fluorocarbon line, trolling with solid Monel or stainless-steel wire line, and trolling with stainless-steel cable line. Each type of line is used for different applications.

Trolling while using monofilament, fluorocarbon, or Dacron line is by far the most popular. Many trollers double the last 3 to 6 feet of the terminal end of their line, using a surgeon's loop, as the terminal end is more susceptible to abrasion. A Sampo ball-bearing swivel, bead-chain swivel, or Spro barrel swivel is then tied to the loop using a uniknot. In trolling, more than any other type of fishing, using a quality swivel that works smoothly is extremely important. No matter how careful you are while trolling, there are times when an acceleration of speed—either to better position the boat while stemming the current, or while making a turn—may cause your lures to spin. If your swivel isn't functioning properly, the end result will be a twisted mess.

Because you're generally probing mid- to moderate depths when trolling, a torpedo-shaped trolling sinker is helpful in presenting your lures. Weights range from ½ through 2 ounces for shallow-water applications, while in deeper water along the surf, in the open reaches of the ocean or sound, or while trolling above lumps, ridges, and rocky outcroppings, you may use trolling sinkers ranging from 3 to 8 ounces to reach the desired depth.

Planers may also be used. These are a combination of a trolling weight and a stainless-steel delta-winged planer designed to take the lure into the depths. The planer has a trip mechanism that is activated when a fish strikes, relieving the pressure on the planer and enabling you to fight the fish without the planer's resistance.

Rather than use trolling sinkers to reach the desired depth, you may employ downriggers, which are mounted on the gunwale of the boat at the stern. Downriggers are really little more than a large reel that holds a heavy stainless-steel cable, which in turn is sent into a selected depth via a heavy, torpedo-shaped lead weight.

Attached to the weight is an outrigger clip to which your line is snapped; upon receiving a strike, this is released, enabling you to fight the striper unencumbered by the weight of a sinker. A depth counter on the downrigger enables you to position the trolling weight, and in turn the lure, at the exact depth you wish it to be fished.

When a trolling sinker or planer is used, it is snapped to the coastlock snap on the swivel, followed by a leader. If you employ a downrigger, snap the leader directly to the coastlock snap of the swivel.

Few will dispute the effectiveness of fluorocarbon leader material, as its refractive index makes it invisible in the water. This is particularly important in shallow water, and in recent years I've chosen to use it in all fishing applications because it gives me an edge over other types of leader material.

The length of the leader depends upon the fishing you're doing. In shallow water with a light popping outfit, some anglers use just a 4-foot length of leader. When employing planers or downriggers, it's not unusual for some anglers to use 12- to 20-foot-long leaders. Personally, I don't like the long leaders: As you lead a fish to the boat, it becomes necessary to handline it the final 12 to 20 feet before you can bring it aboard.

My choice of leader length is in the range of 6 to 8 feet. This enables you to reel the fish in until the swivel reaches the tip-top of the reel, which on most boats puts it well within range of the person who will net the fish to bring it aboard. This completely eliminates the need to handle the leader.

A good rule of thumb is to use leader material that has an approximate breaking test not quite double that of the line you're using. For a popping outfit, that means 20-pound-test leader material, or 40- or 50-pound-test leader material with a heavier outfit. With the heavier leader you're able to easily lift fish aboard without fear of the leader breaking. This is especially helpful if the fish is to be released, and it eliminates the need of a net.

You may tie the leader to the coastlock snap using a uniknot or surgeon's loop. At the terminal end of the leader employ a sturdy duolock or coastlock snap, both of which are strong and enable you to change lures with ease. Avoid a snap swivel at the terminal end of the leader, as you don't want excessive hardware to inhibit the action of the lure.

TROLLING LURES AND RIGS

The troller can use practically every lure ever designed to successfully bring stripers to the boat. But as a practical matter it's best to include in your kit a basic selection of lure types, and to master their use. Having a huge assortment of lures, and constantly changing in the hope of scoring, often results in wasted effort. Veteran trollers develop that sixth sense of knowing just which lure to use given a set of conditions. They develop that important confidence in what they're doing, knowing it consistently brings results.

Within the broad spectrum of lure types effectively used by trollers are leadhead jigs, plugs, plastic- and feather-skirted trolling heads, spoons, metal squids, and a wide variety of tube lures and soft plastic baits designed to resemble specific baitfish. The majority of these lures are trolled by attaching them directly to the snap at the terminal end of the leader.

There are, however, several terminal rigs that use more than one lure in the pattern. By far the most popular is the umbrella rig. It is made of stainless steel in much the same manner as an umbrella frame (hence the name). The umbrella rig may have as few as four arms, with a hard or soft plastic bait on each arm and a single lure dropped 3 to 4 feet down the center of the umbrella. Some umbrella rigs have upward of eight arms, with two lures attached to each arm and a single lure dropped from the center of the umbrella. Depending on the manufacturer, each of the tube or soft lures attached to the arms of the umbrella may have a hook in it, although some may not. Often this results in hooking several fish at one time. Just the weight of the umbrella rig and its multiple baits make it a very heavy rig to use, and while it's popular in some circles, it's not a rig I'll often employ.

The coat hanger rig is designed, as you might guess, much like a coat hanger. A 3- to 4-foot leader runs down the center of the rig, with a single lure at its end. On each end of the coat hanger another lure, usually a tube lure or soft plastic bait, is attached.

With both umbrella and coat hanger rigs the theory is that multiple lures swimming through the water resembles a small school of bait, and that the fish zero in on the trailing bait, with additional strikes coming to the lures as other fish excitedly home in on the rig as it's trolled along.

Dating back many years, the "junk lure" was the predecessor to the umbrella and coat hanger rigs of today. It consisted of a combination of trolling feathers, cedar jigs, and plastic tubing attached to a leader and spaced at 1-foot intervals, usually with a bucktail jig and pork rind as the trailing lure. It was not uncommon to rig six or eight lures on a single leader. Today this rig is more commonly referred to as a daisy chain.

Trollers employ a variety of plugs. The most popular is the subsurface-swimming plug, with its metal or plastic lip drawing it into the depths and providing a side-to-side swimming action. Subsurface swimmers range in length from 2 to 10 inches and are beautifully painted to simulate every baitfish on which the striper feeds. Some plugs are painted pure white, black, yellow, or a combination of all colors in the rainbow. This gives testament that the color may not be important as the action, and as properly presenting it where the stripers are feeding. Suffice it to say that a hungry striper finds it difficult to ignore a plug that looks like something to eat.

The second most popular plug in the troller's arsenal is the popping plug. This floats on the surface and has a concave head, which when trolled pushes water ahead of it. Working the rod tip as it's trolled will enhance its action. This causes the plug to "pop" and churn water ahead of it, then falter until it's "popped" again. This technique is especially effective where rocks, ledges, pilings, or underwater obstructions prevent normal trolling of subsurface plugs—particularly along the submerged rocks of groins that extend seaward and where stripers often congregate.

Rattle plugs, mirror plugs, and darters may also be brought into play while trolling. Each has a distinctive, shimmering action all its own.

Leadhead jigs, as their name implies, have a lead head molded around an O'Shaughnessy-style hook. Trollers employ models weighing a scant ½ ounce with a size 1/0 hook, on up to 3- or 4-ounce jigs with a size 7/0 or 8/0 hook. Leadhead jigs are painted every color in the rainbow, and in some cases carefully airbrushed to replicate a specific baitfish. Still others are unpainted, with a dull black lead finish.

The lead heads are dressed with bucktail skirts, feathers, or soft plastic tails. Many anglers enhance their action by adding a strip of pork rind to the lure when it is trolled.

The parachute jig has a tail made of long, thin plastic hair, approximately 8 inches in length, which is tied around the shank of the jig at its tail. It is tied midway in the length of the fiber, so that when drawn through the water, the hair that lies flat on the head of the jig folds over and streams astern. The parachute jig is dressed with a 4- to 8-inch-long piece of pork rind, and is especially effective worked just off the bottom. Jigging action is imparted by sweeping the rod tip forward, causing the jig to dart ahead and falter, then dart ahead again and falter, as the boat slowly trolls over productive bottom or stems the current in a rip.

A wide variety of plastic- and feather-dressed trolling heads also accounts for many stripers annually. Unlike leadhead jigs, which have their eye on the top of the head for attaching the lure, trolling heads have a hole through the center through which the leader is

Leadhead jigs with the skirt material tied on backward are called parachute jigs, for when trolled the skirt material balloons enticingly as the lure is jigged. A strip of red pork rind adds to its appeal.

attached. They have no side-to-side action, but run straight when trolled. Most have chromed heads with beaded eyes, along with skirts of red and white, black and white, yellow, blue, or green feathers or soft plastic tails. They're available in models ranging from 3 to 6 inches in length.

Spoons are fabricated from sheet metal, and take on the shape of a fish. They're usually made of stainless steel, and are unpainted, or painted all-white, red and white, chartreuse, or yellow. The small, 3- to 6-inch-long models work well when any of the small baitfish such as mullet, spearing, anchovies, and other silvery forage are plentiful.

Bunker spoons were designed primarily to resemble an adult menhaden, and measure in length anywhere from 8 to 12 inches. They have a keel of lead that is fastened to the bottom of the spoon. Most have a size 12/0 or 14/0 O'Shaughnessy hook, with a free-swinging 4/0 or 5/0 treble hook trailing from the J curve of the primary hook. The treble hook actually hooks the majority of the stripers, which wildly strike at this lure. It has a very violent side-to-side swimming action as it is trolled.

While initially found to be very effective when stripers are feeding on adult mossbunker, the bunker spoon also proves extremely

A wire-line trolling outfit such as this, along with the selection of lures displayed, is used wherever stripers are found. The key with wire line is that it gets the lures down into the depths, which is where the stripers most often feed.

effective wherever stripers are feeding on large forage, such as mackerel, herring, and hickory shad.

Under the broad category of metal squids are included such popular lures as block tin squids, hammered stainless-steel jigs, and the wide range of lead squids molded to replicate small forage species. Block tin squids are molded in a wide variety of shapes and sizes; most have a keel with either a fixed or free-swinging hook and a feather or bucktail skirt. Sizes range from 1 to 3 ounces, with size 5/0 through 7/0 O'Shaughnessy hooks most popular. Many anglers add a strip of pork rind to the hook to add to the lure's appeal.

Hammered stainless-steel jigs such as the Hopkins Shorty or No-Eql have for years produced many great catches of stripers. Also gaining in popularity is the multitude of molded lead lures that closely resemble a mullet, anchovy, sand eel, spearing, or other forage and are airbrushed in painstaking detail.

Tube lures, as their name implies, are made of vinyl or plastic tubing. The most basic lure consists of an 8- to 24-inch-long piece of ½- to 1-inch-diameter tubing. The leader is passed through the tubing, and a single size 7/0 through 9/0 O'Shaughnessy hook is tied to it. When this is trolled, water passes through the tubing, and it moves through the water in a slithering, squirming action that

Plastic tube lures trolled deep with the aid of wire line annually account for many stripers throughout their entire range. When fishing with wire line, the key is having the line length marked at 50-foot intervals, so that you can return the lines to the same depth where strikes have been received, usually just off the bottom.

many feel resembles an eel. Among the most popular colors are black, maroon, green, and purple.

Variations on the tube lure include the Bingle Banana, developed by my good friend Don Bingler many years ago, which has a torpedo-shaped molded lead head, with a size 7/0 or 8/0 hook molded securely in the lead. Some tube lures are jointed, with a swiveling tail section.

Plastic bait tails, molded in the shape of forage species, with coloration to match and hooks drawn within the soft plastic, also account for many stripers as they're trolled at various depths.

Another very effective trolling lure is the rigged eel. It's actually part lure and part bait. The lure part consists of a metal squid molded of block tin. A size 7/0 or 8/0 O'Shaughnessy hook with a turned-up eye is molded into the squid. A dead eel, measuring anywhere from 6 to 18 inches, is rigged by running a piece of Dacron line through its mouth, exiting just behind the anus. A size 7/0 or 8/0 O'Shaughnessy hook is tied to the end of the Dacron line, and the hook is then pulled into the body of the eel. The head of the eel is then impaled on the tin squid by running the hook into the eel's lower jaw and exiting through its upper jaw. The Dacron line is then tied to the eye of the tin squid's hook, which protrudes from the top of the squid. For the next step, use a needle and dental floss to tie the eel's mouth shut. Tying a dental floss harness securely around the eel's head where the hook runs through, with a final tie of dental floss around the eel where the hook exits behind the anus, completes the rigging.

Rigged in this manner, the block tin squid with its keel gives the eel an enticing side-to-side swimming action as it's trolled through the water. Eels rigged in this manner may be kept for months at a time in a heavy brine solution made of kosher salt and fresh water. When kept in the heavy brine the eels become very stiff, but after a few minutes of trolling they'll soften up and work perfectly.

TROLLING TECHNIQUES

Armed with a reasonable selection of the lures just discussed, your next objective is to determine just where to troll them. As noted at the outset, it's wise to enlist the services of a guide or charter boatman if you're a newcomer; in just a couple of days' fishing you can observe and experience firsthand the techniques to use and areas to fish.

The next best bet is to obtain NOAA charts of the areas you plan to fish, for they'll give you valuable insight into the bottom configuration of the area. You'll see submerged ridges, ledges, and rock formations; where points of land are located, you'll be certain to find that a rip line forms at a particular stage of the tide. The charts will clearly identify water depth, which helps you decide whether it's best to troll with monofilament line, or if wire line or stainless-steel cable would be a better choice.

Regardless of where you fish, you'll find it usually becomes unmanageable with more than 150 feet of line. I plan my choice of tackle using this as a basis. In the protected reaches of bays and rivers with 5- to 8-foot depths, when using popping outfits, I'll often troll with 75 to 100 feet of line. If I'm probing 15 to 20 feet of water in the ocean, along the surf, or on a broad expanse of bay, I'll extend the length of line and add sufficient weight to get my lures to the desired depths. This often means letting out line until you feel the sinker bounce bottom, then taking up a couple of turns of the reel handle, which lifts the sinker and trailing lure just off the bottom and prevents it from becoming fouled.

When fishing where there's a very strong current, in water of 20 feet or deeper, then the choice of necessity often becomes wire line. Here, too, the length of the wire, coupled with the weight of the trolling sinker, will determine at just what depth the lures will be working.

I've often been asked precisely how to determine the depth at which lures will work. I've seen many formulas—"x number of feet of line will get your lures x feet deep." While formulas sometimes are close, more often than not conditions dictate the best approach to take. When there' a very strong wind and equally strong current working in unison, your lures occasionally will be resting on the bottom and not moving at all if you're trolling at a very slow speed. You've got to have the feel that your lures are working properly, and this often necessitates advancing the throttles. Watch your rod tips, and you'll often see them pulsating from the action of a bunker spoon, swimming plug, or metal squid. When the rod tip is listless, you know something has to be done, and it's usually a speed adjustment, with the general range of 3 to 6 knots being the favored range. A good practice is to watch your lures carefully under a variety of conditions, note the rpms that your tachometers display, and adjust to those speeds under a given set of conditions.

While trolling into the tide or stemming the tide in a rip line requires a certain speed, when you troll with the current you'll have to advance your throttles quite a bit so that your boat and lures are moving faster than the current. Here, too, if you're moving too slowly, the lures will just move listlessly through the water, and you won't get strikes.

In some areas, such as open water, where bait is scattered over a wide area and you pick up readings of stripers at varying depths, you can often use a leisurely, straight-line trolling approach. If strikes aren't forthcoming, it's often wise to adjust your trolling pattern by making leisurely turns, which causes the outboard lures to move faster and rise to the surface on the turn, while the inboard lures travel slower and drop closer to the bottom. Sometimes when you begin to straighten from a turn, the lures will receive strikes, the changes in their speed and depth being the determining factor.

Exciting trolling opportunities are available wherever a rip line forms. A churning rip often develops where there's a point of land, and water flowing around it, on either an ebbing or a flooding tide. Sometimes the rip forms where the current clashes with a lump of high bottom, a sandbar, a submerged rock ledge, or just a collection of boulders scattered about the bottom.

The current often pushes forage along, with shrimp, crabs, squid, and schools of spearing, sand eels, mullet, and other forage being swept along the rip line. Stripers know the food will be carried their way, and they take up station adjacent to the rip, moving in and out to take a morsel of food swept their way.

Trollers who master the technique of pointing their bows into the current and cautiously moving along the edge of the rip line, trolling their lures astern in what sometimes becomes a churning maelstrom, with waves in the rip 6 to 8 feet in height, often enjoy phenomenal results. This fishing requires constant attention at the helm, for you can broach easily. The key is maintaining position, where the swift current is providing the action to your lures.

Stemming the tide with swimming plugs, bucktail jigs, leadheads with plastic bait tails, tube lures, or spoons, will work effectively.

The single lure that most consistently brings strikes when stemming the tide along a rip line is the leadhead jig. The key is to stand in the stern of the boat, with your rod tip pointed down toward the water, and to face aft. Vigorously sweep your rod tip forward, causing the jig to dart ahead, then falter and flutter in the current as it's swept back; repeat the procedure as soon as the line comes taut. Often you can stem the tide in one position and hook up repeatedly by jigging while all other techniques and lures fail to draw a strike.

Trolling along the surf has produced exciting results for me in every Atlantic coast state where stripers are found. Bass often feed right among the churning breakers, for that is where the waves expose sand bugs, crabs, and clams, and where baitfish seek what little sanctuary the shallows offer.

Surf trolling requires lots of attention, particularly among the rock piles on the south side of Montauk, where bass feed among the huge boulders that dot the bottom landscape. Even along Maine's rocky promontories care must be exercised if you troll beyond the crashing breakers.

Stripers often take up station to feed along a rip line. The rips form wherever there is a point of land, or a steep drop-off, where an ebbing or flooding tide clashes with a shallow bar. Forage such as crabs, shrimp, and small baitfish are often carried to the rips by the current, and stripers stem the tide to feed. Care should be taken when stemming the tide, as the rips can become very rough. Ideally, keep your boat out of the rough water and stem the tide, placing your lures in the churning rip.

Along the Jersey and Delmarva coasts, and especially off the surf of the Carolinas, you'll experience many bar formations. While some stripers feed inside the bars in the sloughs favored by surfmen, this is water where boatmen can't venture. They must concentrate their efforts in the waters outside the bars, where trolling can be very pleasant, providing you pay attention to waves approaching from offshore.

Trolling outside the bars is often straight-line trolling, keeping just enough distance to be safe from waves that might otherwise broach you. Keep in mind that wave heights build as they approach the offshore bars, cresting before they crash across the shallow sandbars.

In most surf trolling situations, you'll do well to use monofilament or Dacron line, with the aid of trolling sinkers, as the water usually isn't very deep, and you can enjoy maximum sport without having to go to wire line.

Rigging for wire-line trolling requires a bit more attention than simply spooling monofilament or Dacron line on your reel. The majority of wire-line trollers spool 30- or 50-pound-test Dacron line to their reels but leave sufficient room for a shot of 150 to 200 feet of 30- or 40-pound-test solid Monel or stainless-steel trolling wire.

Pete Casale just netted this husky striper for Ken Schultz, Field & Stream's *Fishing Editor, who hooked it on a parachute leadhead jig and strip of pork rind while trolling aboard the Mistress Too, off Montauk Point, New York. The key to catching big stripers is in getting the lure deep while trolling, which is best accomplished with wire line.*

The standard method of attaching the wire line to the Dacron is to use an Albright knot. However, with the advent of the very small and extremely strong Spro barrel swivels, some anglers now tie the swivel directly to the end of their Dacron, and then use a haywire twist to attach the wire line to the swivel. The swivel is small enough to travel through the ring guides of the rod with ease, provided that you point the tip of the rod in the direction of the line as you retrieve, thus permitting the swivel to travel through unimpeded.

Trolling wire as just described finds popularity in the rips of the Elizabethan Islands of Massachusetts, such as Cuttyhunk, Nantucket, and Martha's Vineyard. It's a religion at Montauk, New York, and used extensively off Sandy Hook, New Jersey. Moving south, where stripers often frequent the 50- and 60-foot depths a half to a mile offshore, many big bass are taken all the way south to the Delmarva Pensinsula, especially trolling big plugs, bunker spoons, and tube lures.

Wire line is particularly effective in taking big bass because they are often feeding well off the beach in deep water—where big menhaden, mackerel, herring, hickory shad, and even small weakfish and bluefish become part of their diet. The wire, coupled with a trolling weight, or sans wire using a downrigger, presents the lures at the depth in which the forage is plentiful and the big stripers feed.

A style of wire-line fishing that differs markedly from using Monel or stainless-steel wire is popular throughout the Chesapeake Bay region, and had its birth around the Chesapeake Bay Bridge and Tunnel complex. It entails using stainless-steel cable, as opposed to solid Monel, which is spooled on level-wind reels. Even the terminal rigging employed is different, with a bucktail jig streamed off what might well be termed a conventional-style bottom rig.

I was first exposed to this technique years ago while fishing at the two main shipping channels, literally situated over tunnels in the bay's floor. The technique is to use an 8- or 10-ounce dipsey-style sinker attached to a three-way swivel via a 3-foot-long leader, to probe the depths over the tunnel tubes. Here the stripers congregate to feed on the forage being swept along and trapped in the rips and eddies formed by the rocky bottom.

To the remaining eye of the swivel a 10-foot-long monofilament leader is tied, with a small leadhead jig and strip of pork rind or plastic tail. The rig is lowered to the bottom and slow-trolled.

You've got to be alert and just keep the sinker bouncing; too much line will result in your snagging bottom. It's a neat way to troll irregular bottom, for as you begin trolling along the shallows, you keep relinquishing line and bouncing the sinker as the water gets deeper. Then, as you approach the shoreline where the tunnel exits and the water begins to get shallow, you have to retrieve line, all the while bouncing the sinker and giving an enticing action to the trailing bucktail jig.

Virginia Beach regulars prefer to use stainless-steel cable, as they find it's more manageable for this type of fishing than single-strand wire; 30- or 40-pound-test cable is favored. Because stainless-steel cable, which is multistrand, occasionally has a strand break, it's extremely important to wear a leather thumb guard when permitting line to flow from the reel. In the event of a strand break, the resulting burr of wire can inflict serious injury to a thumb without a thumb guard.

This technique of using wire is practiced in many of the deep-water areas of the Chesapeake Bay and its tributaries. In shallow water anglers switch to monofilament lines but continue to use the dipsey sinker, three-way swivel, long leader, and bucktail jig–pork rind combo to good advantage. The rig proves especially effective in areas with irregular bottom depths, but requires someone to constantly hold the rod, all the time monitoring the bottom, so the sinker keeps bouncing and the lures keep working enticingly.

I've employed this rig while using both cable and monofilament line in the 20- to 40-foot depths off Island Beach State Park during late fall when migrating stripers gather there to feed on the abundance of sand eels. I suspect I scored particularly well with this rig because I was the only one of a hundred boats that was using it. Most were jigging solid Monel that was essentially fished at approximately the same depth, presenting their lures in the same manner. My cable wire and jigging the dipsey–bucktail combination may have presented the offering to fish that never got to see the jigs fished conventionally.

It's wise to always be alert to the direction the current is moving, which may be a result of tidal flow or extreme wind conditions that counteract normal water movement in an area. Stripers normally move into the current as they feed, and as you troll you'll usually receive most of your strikes when moving into the current, although there are exceptions.

By being alert you can capitalize on the striper's feeding habits. Frequently I've trolled a stretch of rip line, hooked several fish, then retrieved my lures, cruised back, and repositioned myself for another set. Sometimes the strikes came as I trolled with the current, and on other occasions while trolling into it. Each day and set of conditions you encounter will be different; you've got to make adjustments in order to score.

Always be alert to the fact that stripers may be bunched up in a small area, so trolling for miles may result in a lot of wasted time over unproductive bottom. It's not always necessary to retrieve your lures to reposition the boat. Don't hesitate to move your throttles ahead, which will pull your lures toward the surface, then make a wide sweep, reposition yourself, and throttle back. Using loran or GPS you can place your lures within a few feet of where strikes were initially received.

Because you've total mobility with a boat, it's wise to keep a log of your activities, and to plan a strategy before leaving dockside. However, there'll be occasions when even with your best-made plans you may fail to yield a strike. That's when it's important to have a contingency plan. I've often run 15 miles with our *Linda June*, all on a hunch, and arrived at a spot where we enjoyed an hour's exciting trolling and boated several nice stripers after an otherwise uneventful day. June often kids me with what has become a quotable quote: "One last cast, one last set while trolling." I can't tell you how many times that "one last set" paid off.

Although the tackle, lures, and trolling techniques discussed in this chapter are for targeting striped bass, species such as bluefish, weakfish, and fluke frequent much the same grounds and readily strike the same lures. Indeed, up until recently, the largest fluke I'd ever landed was while trolling many years ago with the late Captain Otto Reut aboard his *First Timer*. The doormat walloped a rigged eel intended for stripers. Many blues and weaks of respectable size also succumbed to lures intended for striped bass over the years.

I'd love to have a video of the activity on board after a fruitless day of striper trolling. Almost everyone but the helmsman is dozing . . . when suddenly the reel ratchet emits the signal we've awaited all day. Words can't describe the scene that unfolds. That's what striper trolling is all about, often resulting in "one more trolling set" before heading for the dock.

YAMAHA 130

CHAPTER 9

Casting Lures from Boats

Not surprisingly, stripers being as unpredictable as they are, they often take up residence in spots that are impossible to access while using techniques such as trolling, chumming, presenting natural baits, or jigging. Hence the importance of having casting tackle on board to take advantage of those situations where other techniques are negated by one circumstance or another.

In trying to organize my thoughts for this chapter, I recalled a day while fishing the broad expanse of San Francisco Bay with Leon and Emil Adams. The tide was beginning to ebb, which augured well for a pet spot at the Golden Gate Bridge's South Tower.

By the time we reached the tower, the current was boiling and huge, swirling eddies formed on the ocean side as water poured into the Pacific. Positioning the boat's bow to stem the tide, Leon instructed me to cast right into the maelstrom with an Upperman Bucktail jig and to permit it to sink. It took just two casts. I began a whip retrieve . . . and practically had the rod ripped from my hand. Need I say more about the importance of casting as a technique!

Then there was the huge expanse of Lake Marion in South Carolina. Striped bass were chasing herring on the surface, amid massive stump fields that extended up from the bottom. It was difficult to position the pontoon boat among the stumps, but casting popping plugs brought explosive strikes.

Another time, while drifting live mackerel baits off the mouth of the Saco River in Maine, the stripers were giving young-of-the-

Left: Just drifting along and casting with a bucktail jig resulted in this nice striper hooked by the author in the lower reaches of New York Harbor, with the Statue of Liberty a fitting background. Plugs and leadhead jigs also are favorites of casters who drift through known striper haunts.

year herring fits tight to the bank. A switch to rattle plugs began an exciting adventure catching school bass.

What great, exciting, and nerve-racking memories along Montauk's South Shore, where boulders as big as the boat loomed up from the bottom. As the waves crashed over them in a stiff easterly blow, the stripers were boiling among the rocks. It took intestinal fortitude just to stand at the stern, where an accurate cast between the boulders with a Hopkins Shorty brought strikes, as the bass were feeding on sand eels.

The Chesapeake Bay Bridge and Tunnel exists where the broad expanse of the Atlantic and the Chesapeake meet. Where the water pours through the main channels under which the tunnel runs, it's simply impossible to reach the fish in any way other than casting. For often the menhaden move within inches of the rocky riprap lining the shoreline where the roadway begins its descent into the tunnels. Only a deftly placed cast with a darter, popper, or swimming plug against the rocks brings strikes.

I've included this handful of examples to give you a hands-on feeling for the importance of having casting tackle aboard and ready. No matter where I've fished, these casting opportunities have presented themselves. By being prepared the sport has been extraordinary.

Always make it a point to have a couple of outfits rigged and ready for casting opportunities. This gives you a chance to capitalize on a fast-developing situation where there just isn't enough time to begin rigging up.

TACKLE CHOICES

Casting rods measuring 6½ to 7 feet in overall length work nicely from a boat, for they've sufficient length to enable you to punch out a cast. Select a graphite rod rated for lures ranging from ½ through 3 ounces. While this is a wide range, today's quality rods have the backbone to deliver. This enables you to cast everything from tiny plugs and leadhead jigs on up to heavy metal squids and surface-swimming plugs, depending on what the stripers are eating.

Use the type of casting reel that you're most comfortable with, whether it be a spinning mill or a level-wind/multiplying reel. I tend to lean toward lightweight rods and reels, as I feel too many anglers are overgunned, which takes a lot of the enjoyment out of the fishing. A reel loaded with 250 yards of 12- or 15-pound-test line will handle most stripers with ease. If you hook a big one it'll just take a little longer to bring to net—a small problem, given that you've the luxury of fishing from a boat with an opportunity to move after the fish.

I double the terminal end of the line with a surgeon's loop. Then tie a uniknot to attach a 36- to 40-inch-long fluorocarbon leader's Spro swivel, off which hangs a dropper loop. I most often attach a Clouser Minnow saltwater fly to the dropper loop, which is fished as a teaser ahead of my primary lure, regardless of what it may be. You may, of course, use almost any saltwater fly that resembles the forage on which stripers feed as a teaser.

It's good to keep a pair of outfits rigged, one with a leadhead jig and plastic bait tail, or a bucktail jig and pork rind, and the other with either a popping plug or subsurface-swimming plug. In this way you can present a lure whenever the opportunity presents itself.

I always keep a plastic box of casting lures on the console adjacent to the rod rack, so switching lures can be quickly accomplished. Included in the box is a selection of bucktail jigs, and leadhead jigs with soft plastic bait tails. They range in size from ½ through 2 ounces. The bucktail jigs are either solid white, yellow, or red and white, with torpedo and lima bean styles most popular. Hook sizes range from 3/0 through 7/0 O'Shaughnessy. Many of the lead heads

Boat casters employ light casting outfits when seeking stripers, and catch bass of all sizes on the wide variety of lures included here. The key is probing every level of the water column, using surface lures, medium runners, and bouncing bottom with others, until you find the level at which the fish are feeding.

are unpainted, but are rigged with bright, soft plastic tails, ranging from solid white, pink, and yellow to exact replicas of spearing, sand eels, mullet, mackerel, and other forage species on which stripers feed. Lengths range from 3 to 6 inches.

Included are several block tin squids. The short, fat models are often called mullet squids, while the long thin ones are referred to as sand eel squids. Those with a free-swinging hook dressed with either white feathers or white pork rind cast nicely: The dressed hook swings over the squid as it is cast, resulting in less wind resistance. The Hopkins No-Eql and Shorty are favorites for casting, and very effective when rigged with a tube tail and single hook in red, red and white, green, or purple. Jigs molded of lead in the shape of a fish and airbrushed in minute detail to resemble mackerel, sand eels, mullet, and other forage, with a free-swinging size 5/0 through 7/0 O'Shaughnessy hook, also work well, offering little wind resistance when casting.

There are so many varieties and styles of plugs that you have to refrain yourself from getting carried away. I've often succumbed to plug mania, as each season sees a multitude of new offerings, and quite honestly, they'll all catch stripers!

The key is including a moderate selection in your kit. I like to include both small and large wooden surface-swimming plugs, subsurface swimmers, deep-running rattle plugs, darters, and mirror-type plugs. As to colors, I most often use plugs that are airbrushed to resemble baitfish such as mackerel, mullet, menhaden, anchovies, or herring.

There are also colors that don't resemble anything I've ever seen swimming in the water—such as red and white, black, or pink—which occasionally produce great results. Toward that end I believe very strongly that the action of the lure, depth at which it is worked, and manner in which it is retrieved all combine to bring strikes from hungry stripers.

Equipped with this basic selection of casting lures, you'll be prepared for any contingency, ranging from school stripers to heavyweights.

CASTING TECHNIQUES AND STRATEGIES

While earlier I mentioned using casting to meet any opportunities that develop, many boatmen specifically choose casting over other techniques. Casting admittedly requires working all the time. Because of this you'll find that many avoid it, which directly benefits those who do cast, for there is less pressure on spots requiring casting.

A good approach is to take the time to thoroughly document the casting opportunities within range of the port you sail from. Not surprisingly, many boatmen who fail to do this often fish for years without realizing the striper haunts they cruise by without ever wetting a line.

Within minutes of travel time by boat from almost every marina on all three coasts are bridges, and herein rest the first casting opportunities. The bridges may range in size from the Golden Gate, Verrazano, and 17.6-mile Chesapeake Bay Bridge and Tunnel to tiny spans crossing coastal creeks. In the waters surrounding the huge towers, concrete supports, and abutments, the wooden piles that support the structures, and in many areas the adjoining icebreakers, are gathering places for hungry stripers.

Wherever a piling or tower exists, as water approaches it during a flowing tide, the water separates to go around it, and then joins together as it passes. There's a dead spot both ahead of and behind the structure with minimal current, and a striper can wait for a meal to be swept past without expending as much energy as it would in the direct current.

These spots are a natural to cast to. On the upcurrent side of the bridge you need to position your stern toward the structure, so that you can stem the current. This requires someone to be at the helm at all times, for in a swift tideway it's essential to prevent being swept into the bridge. Cast your lure anywhere from straight toward the bridge to off at a 45-degree angle. In the latter case, the lure will be swept toward the structure—much like a struggling baitfish—as you retrieve it.

On the downcurrent side of the bridge, stem the tide by pointing your the bow at the structure; then position your anglers up at the bow. This will require casting either directly at the structure or to either side of its concrete supports. Casts with leadhead jigs directly at the structure will fall into the swirling eddies and begin to sink quickly. These should be retrieved with a whip retrieve, causing the jig to dart ahead and falter, much like a baitfish struggling in the maelstrom.

When you cast up into the current on either side of the structure, the current will immediately begin pushing the lure toward you. This requires a faster-than-normal retrieve speed; otherwise the lure will be listlessly swept along without any action. You should always feel a taut line, along with the weight of the lure or the pulsating of a swimming plug or metal squid.

With the approach of nightfall, stripers may stay in both of these spots as they feed. However, they have a weakness in that they like to take up station along the shadow line that develops from the lights on the bridge. When facing into the current, on the upcurrent side of the bridge, they'll take a position where they stem the tide with their nose literally on the shadow line, watching for any crabs, shrimp, or small fish being swept along with the tide.

Some will also take up station on the downcurrent side of the bridge, positioned in the light, with their nose on the shadow line, and facing into the darkness to await any forage swept under the bridge.

In each instance boat positioning is important. Much the same casting techniques as described earlier apply in this situation. Stem the tide, with anglers positioned to cast up into the current and retrieve the lure back to the fish. Vary your retrieve and cast up and across the current, so the tidal flow pushes the lure toward the shadow line, all the while being retrieved across the current, where it presents a target to any striper stemming the tide on the shadow line.

Fish points of land, ranging from spots that only extend 30 or 40 feet out from the surrounding beach on up to the huge points on peninsulas. Here, too, as the moving water—a result of wind or tidal flow—moves across a point, it develops rips and eddies, or dead spots where stripers take up station to feed.

My first exposure to "tip hopping" occurred many years ago while fishing with Joe Sparrow and Bob Hutchinson out of Saxis, Virginia. It's a small town on Virginia's Eastern Shore, and leaving its harbor you find the broad expanse of the Chesapeake before you. We never moved more than 100 feet from shore. We approached a point, shut down, and permitted the current to carry us along the bay shore, casting to the rips and eddies formed on the downcurrent side of each point of land. Before the day was over we'd landed a respectable catch of stripers and some spotted weakfish that were bigger than the bass!

Casting to the points is especially effective on large bodies of water such as Long Island Sound, where Connecticut and Long Island anglers regularly post fine scores. In open-ocean waters the same is true, particularly where you've got irregular coastline, such as the beautiful water from Casco Bay, Maine, through Portsmouth, New Hampshire.

Many of the smaller bays along the coast also offer superb casting opportunities. Cape Cod abounds with such locations, including Wellfleet Harbor, Barnstable Harbor, Pleasant Bay, and Buzzards Bay. Over the years I've fished these locations using a variety of techniques, and none was more enjoyable than fishing from a small boat, probing the shoreline with plugs and leadhead jigs.

Still another choice casting sport is that practiced by the tinboat crowd, those rugged individuals who launch aluminum boats powered by outboards from the surf. The late Frank Woolner, my mentor at *Salt Water Sportsman* magazine way back in the 1950s, introduced me to Cape Cod by launching from the outer Cape's surf. Using light outfits, we cast to cruising bass that were chasing every kind of baitfish imaginable. The unique part about casting to stripers at this locale was that the nearest harbors were many miles distant; hence we had miles of water to ourselves. Many boatmen from Provincetown and Nauset just couldn't be bothered running along the beach, as they had plenty of fish near their harbors.

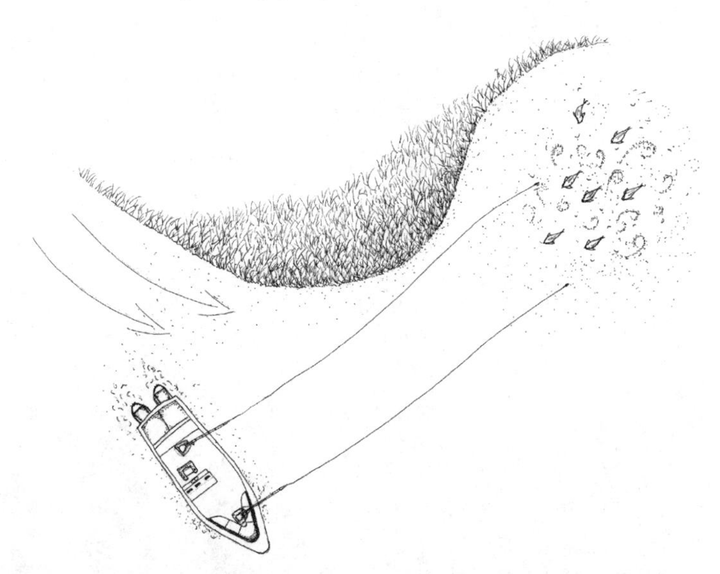

Stripers often take up station at a point of landing, stemming the tide in the rips that form by the moving current. This presents a fine opportunity to move with the current toward the point and cast toward the rip and swirling eddies beyond it, where the stripers are often waiting for forage to be swept their way. If two or three casters are fishing, each should use a different lure, probing the entire water column from the surface to the bottom.

A leadhead jig with yellow plastic tail cast into a school of surfacing stripers brought an immediate strike from this bass. Watch for signs of nervous baitfish schooling on the surface, and of tern, gannet, and gull activity to disclose where stripers are feeding.

While all of the aforementioned techniques provide exciting sport, the casting that really gets the adrenaline pumping is when you see stripers chasing bait on the surface, accompanied by thousands of terns and gulls diving to attack the same bait from the air. Boatmen find that this casting opportunity, affectionately called "chasing the birds," most often exists during the fall. At that time the huge schools of mullet, herring, shad, menhaden, and other forage are leaving the shallow confines of bays and rivers to begin their migrations. The forage moves in huge schools—tens of thousands of fish at times. It's a sight to behold when bait, bass, and birds meet!

The key to chasing the birds is to use a stealth approach. Never, but never speed into a school of surface-feeding stripers. Instead, ease up to the school, judging wind and current to keep you within casting range of the fish, and then shut down and drift. I can't tell you how many times I've seen inexperienced boatmen bore in at full throttle and immediately spook an entire school of fish, completely shutting down the fishing, and spoiling it for everyone.

The ideal situation is when the stripers are chasing bait on top and are receptive to striking a surface lure. That's when the explosive strikes on surface-swimming plugs and popping plugs bring spectacular results. While unlike many game fish, the striper is not a known jumper, when it's chasing baitfish on top it gets itself into a feeding frenzy, often leaping into the air to crash down on a plug.

If your presentation isn't perfect the striper will soon let you know, for often I've had a bass boil behind a plug half a dozen or more times, following all the way to the boat but never once striking the lure. Then again, the next cast brings an explosive strike.

Despite their being in a feeding frenzy when they're on top and into menhaden, mullet, or anchovies, they are sometimes leery of striking a plug. That's when it's time to switch over to a leadhead jig and plastic bait tail, casting out, permitting it to sink, and then retrieving with a whip retrieve. A block tin squid or Hopkins worked at intermediate depths is also very effective at times.

Although there's a tendency to cast into the school of baitfish, keep in mind that stripers are often cruising along the perimeter. They're looking for injured or disoriented fry, and placing several casts out and away from the main commotion will often result in an immediate strike.

Stripers also have a habit of congregating along rocks, ledges, or lumps of high bottom. They do so because that's where the bait tends to congregate. Such spots are readily observed on coastal charts. One spot that immediately comes to mind is the Shrewsbury Rocks, a natural underwater rock pile that extends off the north Jersey shoreline.

The "Rocks" are a tough spot to troll, for any miscalculation will get your lures hung up on the peaks that extend up from the bottom. It's an ideal spot for casting, however, as you can just shut down along the perimeter of the rocks and drift while blind casting to water that you know regularly holds a resident population of fish throughout the summer, as well as being a holding spot for migrating fish due to the abundance of natural forage. Here, too, it pays to work a variety of lures, especially if the fish aren't showing on top, so that your lures are presented throughout the water column.

Still another exciting and fun-filled experience is casting to the tips of the thousands of groins and jetties that extend seaward all along the coast. Stripers take up residence among the tumbled rocks of these structures, for they know that forage traveling along the beach must of necessity go around the front, where they're waiting.

Casting to the jetty fronts can be tricky business, however, and requires someone at the helm at all times, positioning the stern within casting distance of the foaming white water as waves crash across the jetties. I've enjoyed best results while using surface-swimming plugs and popping plugs while casting to the jetty fronts. The key with the big surface-swimming plugs is to use a slow, lazy retrieve, to resemble a big menhaden, hickory shad, or herring swimming away from the rocks. If there's a bass there, it'll nail the plug in an instant.

With popping plugs, try not to be overly aggressively while "popping" the plug with your rod tip. Just flip your rod tip lightly, causing the plug to gurgle and pop as it pushes water ahead of its concave head. Here, too, sometimes the bass will crash it in an instant, but at other times they may follow all the way to the boat, swirling under it repeatedly and turning away at the last minute. Most often strikes will be received with the first couple of casts to a jetty front. If none are received, don't waste a lot of time; just move on to the next jetty and keep casting. Don't hesitate to revisit the jetty front a couple of hours later, for often the bass are moving about and will relocate to a choice spot.

Still another exciting casting opportunity exists while fishing the warm-water discharges of the hundreds of power-generating stations along the coasts. Baitfish tend to congregate in the areas of warm water, and the stripers are not far behind. Each power plant differs in how it discharges water. The prime similarity is that of huge quantities of water flowing into a river, discharge channel, or open bay.

The strong flow of discharge water, clashing with the normal flow of a river caused by tidal flow, forms a maelstrom of churning water and forage. A good approach is to stem the tide, well off from the discharge and in the main flow of current. Cast close to the concrete piping of the discharge, or the rocks that are often along the perimeter. The minute your popping plug or surface-swimming plug touches down, begin your retrieve, for the fast water will be quickly pushing it downcurrent. Make several casts to the outflow pipe. If you hook a fish, don't try to horse it against the competing currents. Slowly ease offshore, take the boat out of gear, and move downcurrent with the fishing, repositioning as necessary. With the fish boated, move back up to the discharge pipe and repeat. Sometimes you'll hook several big stripers where they're tightly schooled up at one pipe, as that's where the bulk of the forage is located.

Some power-generating stations have a whole series of warm-water discharge pipes in a row, and you can systematically fish them by positioning your boat off each one, stemming the tide, and casting. I've seen times when the fishing was torrid; with the tide approaching slack we just dropped the anchor and were able to strategically place casts to the half dozen or more outlet pipes that were in casting range.

While admittedly the most exciting sport is via popping and surface-swimming plugs, with the resultant surface strikes, you can often score with bucktail jigs, leadhead jigs with soft plastic tails, and metal squids, so don't hesitate to change lures if one type isn't producing.

The warm-water discharge of power-generating stations has caused some stripers to alter their migration patterns. They take up residence around the outflows during late fall, and literally spend the winter in the warm water. This often results in good fishing opportunities throughout the Northeast when the snow is falling!

As you develop casting skills, you invariably develop a file of locations that provide great casting opportunities. Often the ocean may be completely unfishable due to a coastal storm, while protected bay and river waters provide an ideal setting for the many casting options identified herein.

CHAPTER 10

Jigging for Bass

There are often occasions when striped bass take up station at various depths in the water column to feed. The forage on which they're feeding often determines the depth. If menhaden are the target, they'll be in the upper strata; if it's sand eels they're feeding on, the linesiders will be hugging bottom. Sometimes the fish will be stacked very tightly in a relatively small area, which makes it difficult for trollers to target them. This is where vertical jigging pays off, for it enables the boatman to present lures to the feeding fish.

Although spinning tackle may be employed, a multiplying reel on a graphite rod with a somewhat stiff tip is a far superior choice. A rod measuring 6 to 7 feet in overall length and rated for 20-pound-test line, along with lures up to 6 ounces, is well suited to most vertical jigging situations. A level-wind casting reel loaded with 200 yards of 20-pound-test monofilament rounds out the outfit nicely. Some party boat anglers spool 30-pound test, as it's less apt to break should a feisty striper become part of a tangle.

Vertical jigging results in the lure being worked vertically, or as near perpendicular to the bottom as possible. For the most part this rules out using many lures that are popular with casters or trollers, such as swimming plugs, poppers, darters, bunker spoons, or metal squids having a keel.

Left: These happy anglers used light spinning tackle to probe the depths of the East River just off from Manhattan. For deep-water situations, a leadhead jig with plastic bait tail, plus a teaser, makes an excellent combination, as the lure gets down in the depths quickly.

JIG SELECTION

The time-proven vertical jigging lures encompass the classic diamond jig and leadhead bucktail jig, plus the many offshoots and variations on these two basic lure types.

The four-sided diamond jig, such as the Ava, is most often molded of lead and chrome plated. A variation includes the Vike, or trisided jig, and jigs such as the Hopkins Shorty and No-Eql, made of hammered stainless steel. There are also many jigs available that are molded of lead or tin to replicate a small baitfish such as a sand eel, spearing, or mullet and airbrushed in minute detail with respect to color and detail.

The majority of these jigs, which are used to seduce a variety of fish, come equipped with treble hooks. For our purposes in seeking striped bass, where undersized fish often have to be released, it's best to remove the treble, or to purchase jigs that have a single hook as standard. While just a plain single O'Shaughnessy-style hook often works fine, I have found that a hook with a plastic tube tail often provides superior action. Carry a selection of colors, including red, purple, green, black, and yellow, for best results. Some anglers dress their hooks with a bucktail or feather skirt, which gives the jig added attraction.

All of the above jigs are available in a variety of weights. To be prepared for all contingencies, it's wise to include jigs ranging from 1 to 6 ounces in your arsenal. Keep in mind that this range of sizes

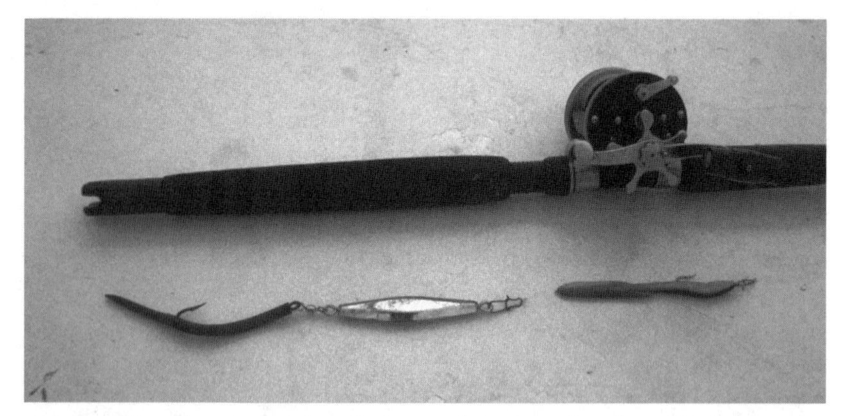

A diamond jig with a plastic tube tail, plus a soft plastic replica of a sand eel fished as a teaser 24 inches ahead of the jig, proves extremely effective when probing the depths. Make certain to work the jig perpendicularly to the bottom, always from the top down and bottom up.

is necessary so that you can work the jig perpendicularly as you drift over a spot. This can't be accomplished if you have a strong wind or drift and are attempting to use a lightweight jig. Under ideal conditions, with nominal drift, you want to match the size of the jig to the baitfish the stripers are feeding on—another reason to keep a variety of shapes and sizes on hand.

The leadhead bucktail jig is without question one of the most effective saltwater lures made. My first magazine article, penned way back in 1953 for *Salt Water Sportsman,* was written to share my thoughts about this versatile lure, which today is just as effective as it was then. Over that span of years, however, the lure has gone through an evolutionary stage. The original bucktail jigs had a skirt of long hair cut from a buck deer's tail and meticulously tied to the jig. Many anglers used feathers, and most garnished the hook with a strip of pork rind for added enhancement.

In the intervening years and with the advent of soft plastics, anglers found it much easier to employ just a plain lead head with a hook molded into it, slipping on a soft plastic bait tail. The late Al Reinfelder and Lou Palma were very instrumental in popularizing the bait tail movement. Also developing potent leadhead jigs was Don Bingler, who used ribbonlike plastic for the bait tail, which streamed behind the hook and worked enticingly as the lure was retrieved.

Today lead heads are molded in a wide variety of shapes and sizes. Many heads are molded to replicate the heads of small forage species, such as a sand eel, mullet, or menhaden. They are beautifully painted in minute detail and look like the head of a live fish. Still, many are left plain, with an unpainted head, depending on the attraction of the seductive soft plastic tail to bring strikes.

The plastic tails used on lead heads are available in literally hundreds of shapes and sizes and in every color of the rainbow. Many are molded to exactly replicate a small baitfish. Others are in outlandish colors such as hot pink, bright yellow, or snow white and really don't resemble anything on which a striper might feed. Still, their combination of color and the action imparted to them as they are jigged brings exciting strikes.

Lead heads are available in a wide range of weights, and most boatmen include weights ranging from ½ ounce up to 4 ounces in their lure box; these easily accommodate most conditions encountered. With both diamond-style and leadhead jigs, hook sizes match the size of the jig. For stripers the preferred sizes usually range from 2/0 through 7/0, with the O'Shaughnessy hook style the most popular.

With the popularity of soft plastic tails, there's less use of pork rind strips than was the case years ago. There are, however, many anglers who swear that the addition of a 4- to 7-inch-long strip of pork rind on their jig hook results in more strikes. The fluttering action as the jig moves to the surface and falters makes it resemble a struggling baitfish, drawing strikes from hungry stripers.

RIGGING JIGS

There are just a couple of basic methods of terminal rigging used when vertical jigging. The most popular—although not the most productive—method is to use a short leader between line and jig. The second method, while more effective, is actually less often used, and is employed with a teaser fished 24 to 36 inches ahead of the jig. Toward that end, I've written perhaps more magazine articles on using a teaser–jig combo than on any other technique I've ever written about. Still, for some reason unknown to me, anglers just don't try this potent method.

For terminal rigging when using a single lure, either a diamond-style or leadhead jig, double a couple of feet of the terminal end of your 20-pound-test line using a surgeon's loop. Then use a surgeon's knot to attach 3 to 4 feet of 30-pound-test fluorocarbon leader material. This heavier-weight leader material will minimize chafing against a big striper's rough mouth or sharp gill plates and scales. If you wish, you can employ a small Spro barrel swivel between line and leader as well.

You can tie the jig directly to the end of the leader using a uniknot, permitting a small loop to remain in the knot by not pulling it up tight against the jig. I like to use a duolock snap, as this facilitates lure changing and avoids the necessity of retying every time I change jigs.

The leader used when fishing with a teaser is described in another chapter, and it works equally well when cast or trolled from boat or beach, so by all means don't hesitate to make this your prime rig when vertical jigging.

The teasers employed when jigging vertically range from daintily tied epoxy-head Clouser saltwater flies tied on 2/0 or 3/0 stainless-steel hooks to a simple tuft of bucktail tied to an O'Shaughnessy hook. Some anglers use a soft plastic bait tail—even the same style and size used on their primary jig—which is slipped onto an O'Shaughnessy hook, usually a size 3/0 through 5/0.

Rigged and ready is the key to successful vertical jigging. Whether you choose to troll, cast, or fish with natural baits, you should always be prepared for times when a vertical jigging opportunity presents itself.

JIGGING TECHNIQUES

Among the best situations to employ this technique is while drifting across a bottom that regularly holds an abundance of forage such as sand eels, herring, anchovies, and mackerel. The forage regularly congregates above patches of rocky bottom, and especially wherever there is a lump or patch of high bottom. The latter are often marked on coastal charts as ridges or banks. The baitfish also collect along rip lines and are often trapped in eddies created when swift currents flow around submerged obstructions, such as wrecks or reefs.

A fishfinder, loran, and GPS are very useful pieces of electronics that will enable you to find precise locations, and then to read whether baitfish and stripers are on a particular patch of bottom. By all means establish a logbook of loran and GPS coordinates. Once you've gained experience, it's wise to move from spot to spot, without wetting a line, until you find concentrations of bait and bass.

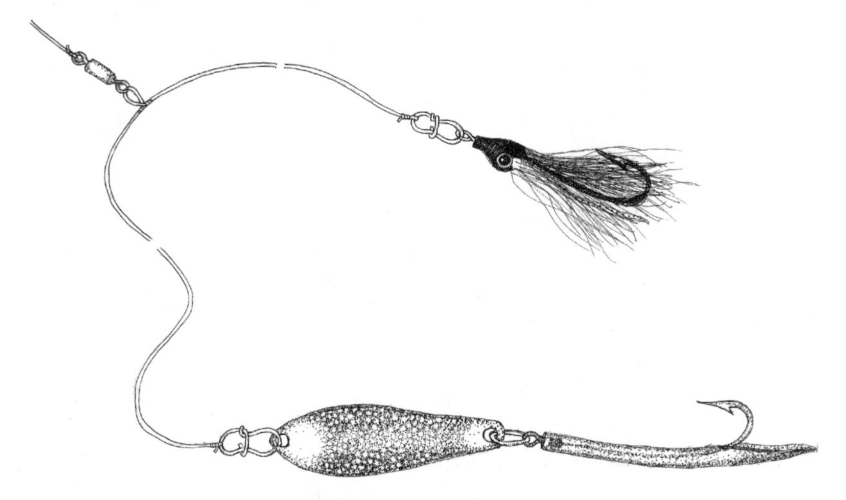

The combination of a stainless-steel jig or diamond jig, with a Clouser saltwater fly fished 24 to 36 inches ahead of it, makes an extremely effective jigging rig. With it you can probe the entire water column from the surface to the bottom and back up again. The basic teaser rig can also be used wherever and whenever you use a lure, be it a plug, leadhead jig, or metal squid, from surf, jetty, bridge, or boat.

When you've found the spot, determine the direction that the wind or current will move your boat, take a position upcurrent from it, and shut down.

The key to successful vertical jigging is to always begin by working the jig from the surface to the bottom, and then back to the surface. In this way you work the lure through the entire range of the water column, both down and up. Once you begin to receive strikes at a specific depth, you can adjust accordingly, concentrating your efforts at a depth where the fish are feeding. This is especially true when you're fishing in 50 or 60 feet of water—you won't have to waste time and effort.

Begin by permitting your diamond or leadhead jig to settle 5 or 6 feet into the depths, place your thumb on the line to stop it, then smartly lift your rod tip, causing the lure to move to the surface, then falter and settle back. Ease your thumb from the line and permit another 5 or 6 feet of line to slip from the spool. Repeat the same procedure. Continue this step until you receive a strike, or feel the jig touch bottom.

Because many bass hug the bottom, it's wise to concentrate some jigging effort there. Lock the reel in gear, reel up 5 or 6 feet of line, and vigorously lift your rod tip, which sweeps the lure toward the surface. Then permit it to settle again, reeling a like amount of line and repeating until the jig is 15 or 20 feet off the bottom. Then place the reel in free spool, and work the jig back down to the bottom.

If you haven't received a strike, jig the lure back to the surface, stopping every 5 or 6 feet until you reach the surface. Then start all over again.

Keep in mind that you want the jig to be working perpendicular to the bottom. If you've got extremely strong current or wind and attempt to use a 1-ounce jig, you'll find that the lure will stream out and away from the boat. This is where it's important to have a wide range of lure weights. Use a sufficiently heavy jig so that your line is practically straight up and down as you drift along.

While jigs up to 6 ounces are usually adequate, I pressed 10- and 12-ounce jigs into use when we drifted over Klondike Banks with 20-knot winds and 6-foot seas. The heavy jigs got to the bottom fast. The stripers were hugging the bottom feeding on sand eels, and strikes came at regular intervals when I just worked the water column from the bottom and up about 6 feet. The jigs held in the strike zone despite the wind and rough water, something that would not have been possible with a lighter-weight jig.

Aboard the *Linda June* we always began our jigging efforts by June using a leadhead jig, while I went with a diamond or stainless-steel jig. Not surprisingly, on some days one lure produced better than another, making it important to begin with a variety of jig types until you find the one the stripers want.

We always had a marker buoy available, too. While the loran, GPS, and fishfinder were helpful to begin with, we found an old-fashioned marker buoy the ideal tool to pinpoint a location where strikes were received. You can fashion one from a 1-gallon plastic milk jug. Spray-paint it blaze orange, which shows up brightly in a rough ocean. I tie a 75-foot-long piece of 130-pound-test Dacron line to the handle of the milk jug, and a 16-ounce sinker to the end.

As soon as a strike is received, drop the buoy over. I use the marker when I'm repositioning the boat, sometimes drifting right back within a couple of feet of the marker, but also working the perimeter, which I've always found easier to do than using the electronics.

While electronics are very useful when the ocean appears devoid of life, you should always be alert for breaking bait, or gulls, terns, and gannets. Often the birds will give an indication of fish feeding in the depths. Just a few breaks on the surface can indicate large concentrations, often way down in the water column.

Here, too, as you slowly approach birds, bait, or breaking bass, don't hesitate to toss a marker buoy and then watch the fishfinder

When you see schools of bait and stripers feeding like this on the surface, you can be sure there are many more feeding in the depths. Probe every level of the water column while vertical jigging; once strikes are received, concentrate your jigging at the depth at which the stripers are feeding.

screen to determine what's going on in the depths. At all costs avoid speeding into breaking fish, which will often spook the school and disperse it. Remember, of course, that for every striper you see on top, there may be hundreds in the depths.

Varying the speed of your retrieve is important, too. While I'm a proponent of working the jig down to the bottom and back up, the speed at which you do this is also important. Historically a slow to moderate jigging speed works best for stripers, with a fast retrieve often resulting in strikes from bluefish in the area.

At times simply permitting the jig to plummet to the bottom may brings strikes as it drops. Here's where it's always important to maintain line control, with your thumb lightly on the spool. Immediately upon receiving a strike, apply thumb pressure to the line, lift back to set the hook, and lock the reel in gear. If a strike isn't received by the time you reach bottom then lock the reel in gear and reel it back to the surface, working your rod tip as you do so.

There are times, however, when speed reeling is what brings strikes. I've even been out there on blitz occasions when everything works, although those days are admittedly the exception.

By all means don't hesitate to experiment with a variety of jigs and teasers, especially if the fishing's slow. I can vividly recall a day when fishing aboard Captain Ed Beneducci's party boat *Marlin VI* off Montauk Point, when the ocean was alive with feeding stripers breaking on tiny anchovies. The fish just wouldn't look at a standard-sized diamond or leadhead jig. A tiny chartreuse-and-yellow Clouser epoxy-head teaser with a trace of silver Mylar, tied on a 2/0 hook, resembled the tiny baitfish and brought strikes until I was arm-weary.

Another time, while aboard the party boat *Gambler* of Captain Bobby Bogan, we were jigging off Seaside Heights, New Jersey. There were no stripers showing on the surface, yet the fish scope in the wheelhouse was lit up with huge schools of sand eels tight to the bottom. That day there were perhaps 20 anglers on board. Using the same jig–teaser combo described earlier, only with a brown-and-white Clouser with gold Mylar, I landed a total of 31 striped bass. It was the most I've ever landed from a party boat on single day, and more than all the other anglers on board landed. What always surprises me when I blitz bass on teasers is that, despite my offering spare rigs to anglers on board, most feel it doesn't matter. By the time they get rigged with a teaser the action may have subsided. That day most of the bass were hooked on the tiny teaser, with several doubleheaders. I kept only one of the bass for the table, and when I cleaned it found its stomach filled with skinny sand eels barely 2 inches long, just the size of the teaser.

I cite these examples not to demonstrate the importance of catching a lot of stripers, which to me is incidental. But on days when the fishing is extremely slow, this technique often puts a striper or two on board when others who fail to experiment may not score at all.

Working your jig perpendicularly to the bottom is important. There are times when, despite using a heavy jig, it's difficult to do. Then an underhanded cast away from the boat, into the direction that the boat is drifting, will help achieve this. As the jig settles to the bottom, the boat catches up with it and you begin your retrieve, achieving line control over the jig.

I've had extremely good results when fishing impoundments such as Lakes Marion and Moultrie and using vertical jigging techniques. Often the stripers would be down near the bottom, feeding on herring and gizzard shad, and they'd respond to a Hopkins jigged right near the bottom.

What I try to avoid at all times is a situation where the jig floats off bottom and balloons to the surface as a result of a fast drift. When this happens, you really have little control of the lure, and while you'll occasionally hook fish, you'll consistently do better when the retrieve is near vertical.

Anchoring is still another option. I've experienced times when a crowd of boats made it difficult to drift a location where fish were pinpointed. Then you should use the same marker buoy described earlier to mark just where the bait and fish are located, and anchor well off from the spot, paying out rode until you're positioned right over the fish. Then employ the same vertical jigging techniques discussed earlier.

Don't hesitate to adjust the amount of rode you use; this will reposition your boat over choice bottom and increase your likelihood of receiving strikes from bass that are moving along the bottom.

Vertical jigging can be tiresome at times. But it is also exciting, especially when a heavyweight wallops the jig and practically rips the outfit from your grasp. It's just one of many techniques that at a given time can be brought into play to produce exciting results.

CHAPTER 11

Fishing Live Baits from Boats

Hardly a season goes by that veteran striped bass anglers don't discuss the merits of lures versus natural baits. Indeed, it's a discussion that will continue ad infinitum, for there's no best approach. Much of it depends on how you like to fish, and there are many who feel fishing with natural baits is more in keeping with the contemplative side of striper fishing.

While there are times when stripers will charge almost any lure trolled, jigged, or cast their way, there are equally as many or more occasions when they'll ignore the best presentation, but readily take natural bait. As I've traveled about, fishing the many impoundments where stripers flourish as well as broad expanses of sound, bay, and ocean waters, I've had many memorable trips thanks to employing the forage stripers are accustomed to feeding on.

Within this chapter boat fishing will be covered in depth, for those who angle from comfortable craft are at a decided advantage. For starters, they can cover a greater range of spots frequented by stripers. Importantly, many bass boats are equipped with live wells that enable anglers to keep baits in prime condition.

My observation has been that striped bass often have to expend a great deal of time finding sufficient food to satisfy their appetites. As such, they're not apt to hesitate when you present either a live or fresh dead bait. Stripers feed on an enormous variety of forage species. At first blush menhaden, clams, herring, and sea worms come to mind. Consider, however, that at one time or another

Left: Live eels often bring fast action from big stripers. Most often they're hooked through the lips or eyes, and sent into the depths with a bottom rig. They're also effective when livelined from a drifting or anchored boat.

striped bass will feed on the fry of almost every bottom feeder and game fish found in their range. I've removed bluefish, weakfish, fluke, bergalls, winter flounder, sea bass, scup, tautog, and croakers from their stomachs on many occasions.

You can add in the customary forage, too—hickory shad, several species of mackerel, herring, mullet, rainfish, spearing, anchovies, sand eels, common eels . . . , the list goes on and on. Don't forget the variety of crabs scurrying along the bottom, including the blue crab, calico crab, and rock crab. Then there are the sand bugs, found buried by the thousands in the sand. Any species of shrimp is a welcome treat, from the tiny grass shrimp found in coastal bays and rivers to the sizable shrimp found in the ocean. Even squid are fair game when stripers are hungry. Sea worms such as the sandworm, bloodworm, tapeworm, and myriad others are a treat to feeding stripers. Hungry stripers equally favor the same mussels and clams you enjoy on your dinner table. I'm certain I've overlooked some of their diet, but you can readily see that a wide range of choices are available to you should you decide to seek old linesides by presenting him with a fresh natural bait for dinner.

There are basically four different methods that boatmen employ to present their natural baits: drifting, anchoring, trolling, and casting. Each has its applications and its devotees.

Drifting is one of my favorite techniques. The key is having an in-depth knowledge of the area you plan to fish. It may be the broad expanse of a coastal bay, an offshore lump of high bottom where bass congregate, or a swift-running tidal river. Each of the aforementioned locales holds bass, but you've got to know at which stage of the tide stripers frequent the area, how the stage of the moon will affect water flow, and whether wind conditions impact the drift. In many areas a spot might be completely void of baitfish or stripers at one stage of the tide, perhaps incoming water, while it teems with activity on the ebb.

Drifting lends itself to light-tackle fishing. For inshore, protected waters where schoolies are most often the target I like to use a popping outfit, moving up to a rod rated for 20-pound-class line on big water, where heavy stripers roam.

Getting to know which spots produce best often takes a great deal of time. Those new to using natural baits can immediately expand their knowledge by seeking the services of a veteran charter boat guide, party boat skipper, or local angler. Be alert to what they do and where they fish, and then replicate it aboard your own craft. I know many guides and skippers who welcome newcomers aboard, for they feel an angler who knows what he's doing and fishing in a fleet is not disruptive, as might be the case of a tyro boatman who impacts the fishing of others, including charter boats.

Perhaps the single most important suggestion I can make to enhance your catch while drifting is to recognize that stripers move in all levels of the water table. Many fish hug the bottom, while others move at intermediate depths, and a limited number show on the surface. I capitalize on this by fishing baits at different depths as I drift along.

A popular striper bait throughout their entire range is the sandworm. They're dug in Maine, air-freighted all along the coast, and readily available at most bait and tackle shops. By my observation many anglers who elect to fish with sandworms fish them either on the bottom or at intermediate depths. They'd be better served to have half the anglers on board fish with bottom rigs and the other half with float rigs, reaching bass anywhere in the water table they may be cruising and feeding.

A fine bottom rig for fishing sandworms consists of tying a small three-way swivel directly to the end of your line. Tie a 6- to 8-inch-long piece of light monofilament to one eye of the swivel, with a loop in its end onto which you can slip a bank- or dipsey-style sinker of sufficient weight to bounce bottom as you drift along. The sinker weight may range from ½ ounce in bay or river waters, to 3 or 4 ounces in deeper sound or ocean waters.

To the remaining eye of the swivel tie a 36- to 40-inch-long piece of 20- or 30-pound-test fluorocarbon leader material. Snell a size 1, 1/0, or 2/0 Claw- or Beak-style hook with a baitholder shank to the leader and you're ready to go.

To bait up, hold the sandworm by its head; when it opens its mouth, insert the point of the hook into its mouth, working the point down into the worm, exiting it about an inch from the head. Then slide the worm onto the shank of the hook, where the barbs of the baitholder shank will hold it securely. Hooked in this manner, the worm will stay alive and swimming for a long while. Large bloodworms may be hooked in the same manner, although some prefer to hook the worm in the middle, with both ends trailing.

Permit the rig to settle to the bottom, and then drift with wind or current over the favored bottom. Lift your rod tip periodically, causing the worm to swim up from the bottom and settle back down in an enticing manner. Most often a striper will inhale the bait as it drifts along, hooking itself as it moves off. Instinctively most anglers lift back and strike the fish when it moves off, with one smart lift of the rod tip being sufficient, as the laser-sharp point of the hook will quickly penetrate. Avoid repeated striking, which does little more than rip a hole in the fish's jaw, and can lead to losing the fish during a sustained run.

Recognizing that some stripers may be feeding at intermediate depths, a float rig should probe the water midway between the surface and the bottom. I double the end of my line using a surgeon's loop, and then use a uniknot to tie a small Spro barrel swivel to the loop. Next comes 36 to 40 inches of 20- or 30-pound-test fluorocarbon leader material, and a size 1, 1/0, or 2/0 Claw- or Beak-style hook with a baitholder shank. In the middle of the leader I'll slip on a rubber-cored sinker of ½ to 1 ounce in weight, which will help hold the line and leader perpendicular to the bottom as it drifts along. If I'm fishing in 15 feet of water I'll position a cork, Styrofoam, or Snap Float about 7 or 8 feet from the hook, which will po-

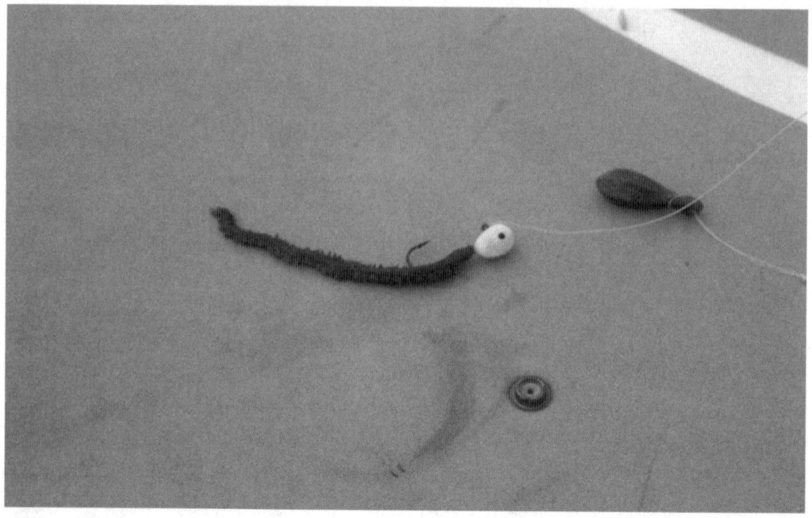

A live sandworm, hooked through the mouth on a floating jig head and drifted along the bottom, works extremely well wherever stripers are found. It is an especially effective rig in bay or river waters, where you can drift through known striper haunts.

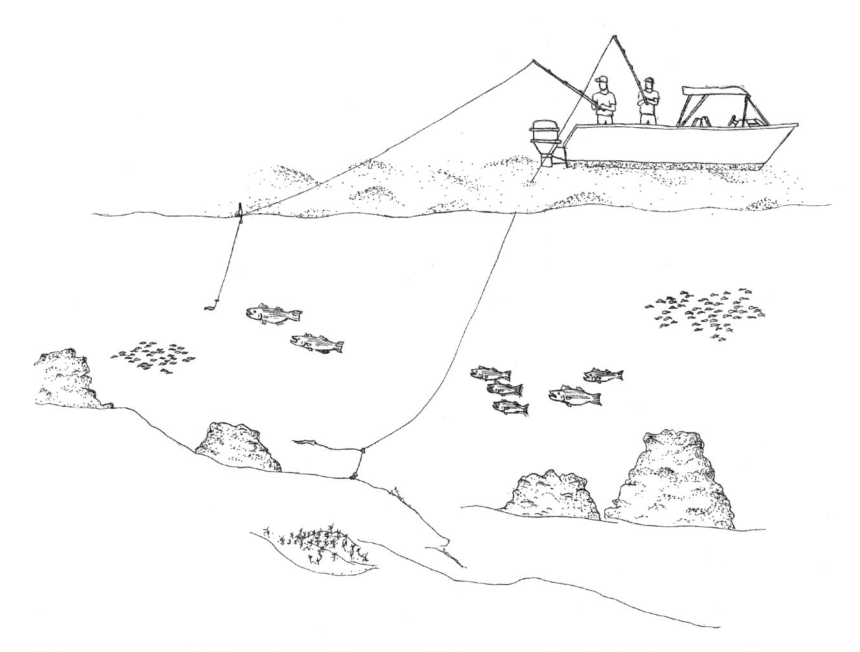

Whenever you're drifting along with natural baits, remember that stripers sometimes are feeding tight to the bottom, and at other times move up through various depths in the water column, depending on the forage in the area. As such it's always wise to fish one rig right on the bottom with a sinker, and to use a float rig to position a bait at intermediate levels. Often the bait suspended at mid-depth will surprise you with the number of strikes it receives.

sition it at midlevel. The worm is placed on the hook in the same manner described earlier, and the rig drifted out 50 to 75 feet from the boat.

With this combination of baits you'll be surprised when at times only the bottom rig scores, and sometimes the float rig, but often it'll be a combination of both that receives strikes as you drift across productive bottom.

At times you can use the same combination of rigs—with a hook size to match the bait being used—hooking live eels through the lips and drifting them along, or using whole squid with their tentacles trailing. A hungry bass would be hard-pressed to pass up any of these baits.

Because many anglers release stripers, you can use the same basic rig and substitute Circle-style hooks, in sizes ranging from 4/0 through 10/0, which makes release easier, as the bass are usually hooked in the corner of the jaw. This dual combination may be used with any variety of large forage species as bait, such as croaker, menhaden, mullet, anchovy, or other baitfish.

In rivers, where there are bridges, docks, and marinas, or where channels are narrow, it sometimes becomes difficult to drift the choice locations, and then anchoring becomes a viable option. Always keep in mind that stripers will take up station to feed where there is minimal current. Plan your anchoring to position your boat so it drifts toward a bridge abutment or icebreaker, for as the current approaches, it will split and cause a dead spot, where the stripers often stem the current and wait for a meal to be swept to them.

On the downcurrent side of a bridge or breakwater, you can anchor so that your baits are fished in the quiet, swirling water of the eddies. Here, too, fish some baits on the bottom and some at intermediate levels. Depending on the tide, and especially as it approaches slack water, you can often remove the float and liveline the bait, permitting it to drift and swim about on its own, until suddenly a hungry striper engulfs it. Soft and shedder crabs are especially effective baits in this kind of situation, for when they shed the crabs are at the mercy of the current, swept along, becoming easy meals for a hungry striper. Don't hesitate to use a whole crab, but to prevent the soft meat from being ripped from the hook, secure it using elastic thread or heavy sewing thread.

Another prime spot to anchor is along the surf. Recognize that stripers, as noted earlier, are almost always moving about. Much like a hunter seeking rabbits along a hedgerow, they move along the surf as they move from one locale to another. Anchor a safe distance off the surf, with your bow pointed seaward toward any incoming swell. Cast your rig in toward the cresting breakers and you'll be placing your baits right where the churning action is exposing crabs, sand bugs, sand eels, and other morsels, and any bass cruising along the beach is apt to find it.

CASTING NATURALS

Casting natural baits is still another exciting option. Use a popping or spinning outfit, and tie a surgeon's loop directly to the end of your line. Then use a uniknot or blood knot to attach 36 to 40 inches of 30-pound-test fluorocarbon leader material. For the majority of live baitfish such as eels, menhaden, herring, mackerel, or hickory shad, a size 5/0 through 7/0 Live Bait, Beak, Claw, or Octopus hook with a plain shank will work fine. If using a Circle hook, size 7/0 through 12/0 is appropriate. A treble hook may also be used, with the 3/0 or 4/0 Mustad Triple Grip a fine choice.

The easiest, and a very effective, way to hook most baitfish is to run the hook through the lower jaw and out the upper lip. With a treble hook, impale the bait with just a single hook, leaving the two remaining barbs to hook the fish. Hooked in this manner, a bait may be cast with ease, and little fear of it being ripped from the hook.

You may also hook fish such as herring and mackerel through the fleshy part of the back, just forward of the dorsal fin. Some anglers will place a hook near the fish's anal fin, with the theory

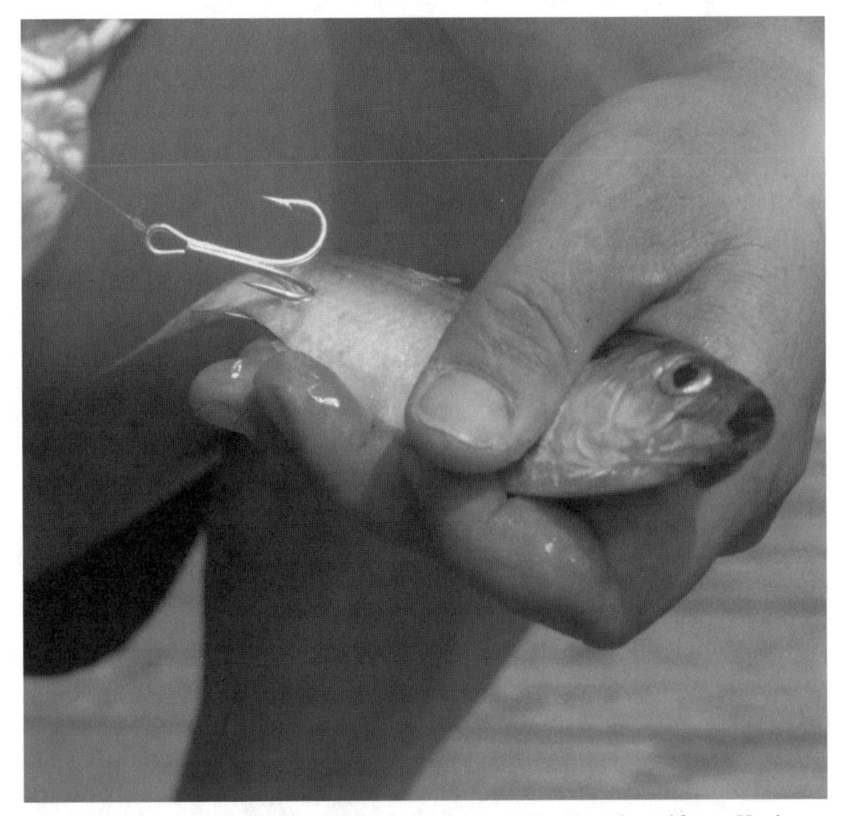

Live herring are an effective striped bass bait wherever stripers are in residence. Herring may be hooked through the lips or just forward of the dorsal fin with a single hook, or impaled with a treble hook as shown.

that a striper ingests the bait headfirst, resulting in the hook being in a good position to penetrate as the fish swallows the bait. You may also place the hook in the back of the fish, behind the dorsal fin, and just forward of the tail. Keep in mind that hooking the baitfish in the flesh may result in it ripping from the hook as you execute a cast, which is why most anglers prefer hooking through the jaw and lip.

Casting live baits is particularly effective where it's otherwise impossible to drift, anchor, or troll. Typical of the spots that regularly hold large numbers of stripers are the seaward sections of the thousands of rock and wood groins and jetties that extend seaward all along the coast, along with natural rock promontories. The same is true of submerged rock ledges, where boulders extend up from the bottom and make a close approach treacherous. The key is positioning your boat with the bow pointed into the approaching waves or swell, and ensuring that someone is at the helm at all times while anglers cast their baits from the stern.

When you cast a live bait to a spot where you expect a striper to be waiting for a meal, permit the bait to swim about freely. The bait will emit distress sounds that stripers immediately pick up and move toward. As a bass does so, the bait, such as menhaden, herring, mackerel, or other fish, will immediately realize it's being stalked, and its movements will be excitedly telegraphed up the line. Your reel should be in free spool and not inhibit the movement of the bait. Often you'll see the baitfish boil to the surface, swimming furiously as it attempts to evade the striper targeting it.

Sometimes a striper will approach and toy with the bait, swimming around and trying to determine whether it should or shouldn't take it. At other times there's no hesitation, and it will in an instant inhale the bait and move off. As it does so, point your rod in the direction the line is moving, permit it to move off for a few seconds, lock the reel in gear, and when the line comes taut and you feel the weight of the fish, lift back smartly to set the hook.

Often you'll spot sizable schools of forage fish such as menhaden, hickory shad, herring, and mackerel in an area. The menhaden normally won't strike a lure, but they can easily be snagged by casting weighted treble hook into the school. You can also snag them using a pair of treble hooks rigged on a leader ahead of a diamond or leadhead jig.

The author used a live croaker as bait to subdue this husky striper. He fished the bait using a bottom rig and Circle hook on the broad expanse of the Chesapeake Bay, the major nursery ground for stripers.

Herring, hickory shad, snapper blues, jacks, and mackerel will readily strike small lures, and you'll enjoy catching them on a multihooked Sabiki rig, or a pair of shad darts or Clouser flies fished as teasers ahead of a diamond or leadhead jig. Just work the combination through the depths, working the rod tip, causing the rig to dart ahead and falter. Often you'll catch the baitfish two or three at a time.

If your boat doesn't have a live well, just catch a few baits and keep them in a 5-gallon bucket of seawater. Take care not to put too many baits in the bucket—they'll quickly deplete the oxygen and die.

Trolling with live baits isn't practiced as much as other techniques, but it's extremely effective at times. The same bottom rig described earlier for sandworms can be trolled through river water, in coastal canals, creeks, and estuaries, and especially in the broad expanse of shallow bays. Trolling is particularly effective when there's no structure and the fish are apt to be spread over a wide area of bottom.

You can add a June Bug, Colorado, or Willow Leaf spinner just ahead of a hook that's baited with a sandworm, with the shiny blades of the spinner providing the sparkle that draws strikes to the trailing sandworm.

You can troll live eels, mackerel, and herring using this technique as well. Always hook baits to be trolled through the lips, so they swim naturally and don't spin as you troll along.

Many veteran anglers take the pains to rig whole squid as trolling baits, and regularly post good scores. Insert a 6/0 or 7/0 O'Shaughnessy-style hook in the head of the squid, exiting the hook 2 inches in back of the head. Then, using a needle, run dental floss through the squid and through the eye of the hook, which is inside the head, and neatly tie it off. When a squid rigged in this manner is placed in the water and trolled along the bottom, it will track straight and not spin, with its tentacles fluttering enticingly as it's trolled along.

When trolling, it's important to be aware of the stage of the tide. Often in the shallow bays behind the barrier beaches—such as are common on the South Shore of Long Island, the length of the south Jersey coast, and along the Delmarva Peninsula—stripers will travel along the channel edges on a flooding tide, moving onto the flats to feed on the abundance of forage such as small baitfish, crabs, and grass shrimp, and then return to the channels as the tide ebbs. By working the channel edges, you can often intercept the stripers as they move from one area to another to feed.

Fishing with natural baits can become an addiction. There's the fun of obtaining the bait. Indeed, over the years I've used eel traps, seines, baited hooks, pitchforks, crab rakes, and jigs to secure a wide variety of baits to present to the princely striper. Finally comes the challenge of either trolling, casting, drifting, or anchoring to present those baits. Most often it was rewarding, and continues to rate as a very effective way of catching stripers of all sizes.

Tom Melton, editor of The Fisherman, *hooked this striper while drifting a live eel from the party boat Sea Otter off Montauk, Long Island. Striped bass are nocturnal feeders and night fishing often produces exciting action.*

CHAPTER 12

Care and Cleaning

The striped bass has a long reputation as a delight on the dinner table. Its firm white meat can be prepared using a wide range of recipes to suit the most discriminating taste. Not surprisingly, however, there have been times when I've been served striped bass that had a flavor that was less than desirable. On some of those occasions I attributed it to the preparation, but more often than not I suspect that the fish was not cared for and cleaned properly.

The proper care and cleaning of your catch should be of paramount concern. Indeed, after you land a striped bass, it is suddenly exposed to a variety of conditions that immediately begin the deterioration process. The two that immediately come to mind are wind and the heat of day. Regardless of whether you're fishing from a boat or the beach, your immediate concern should be to prevent your catch from being exposed to either of these conditions.

There is, however, the basic fact that you've just landed a striper that is still alive. From my observation, most anglers permit the fish to die, and later decide how to care for it. This is perhaps the biggest mistake of all, for this retains all of the blood within the fish, which detracts from the flavor of the fish and may in fact cause it to deteriorate.

By way of comparison, any animal meat that is used for the table, such as chicken, beef, or pork, has been immediately bled. The same should be done with striped bass. It is easily accom-

Left: The key to enjoying the superb flavor of striped bass is properly caring for them from the minute they are landed. This striper was bled, cleaned and iced just a few minutes after being brought aboard, ensuring excellent table quality.

plished while the fish is still alive, as the heart will immediately pump the blood from the fish. This simply requires inserting a knife behind the pectoral fin and making a cut until the blood begins to flow. This simple procedure will drain the great majority of blood from the fish—actually quite a sizable amount. It will be the single best step to ensure that your fish will arrive in the kitchen in prime condition.

As soon as the fish has bled, the next step is to remove its entrails. Many anglers make the mistake of leaving their fish to lie on the beach or in a fishbox for the entire day, cleaning it at the conclusion of their trip. During this time the digestive juices in the fish's stomach continue to work. This in turn causes the meat of the fish to deteriorate, especially if the fish has not been chilled promptly.

Using a sharp knife, insert the point into the stomach at the anus, and cut forward all the way to just forward of the gills. Reach into the stomach cavity, and cut the tube leading from the throat to the stomach. Next, cut the tube that leads to the anus, and remove and discard the entire stomach and its contents. Rinse the stomach cavity in seawater. Your striper is now ready for ice.

By the way, over the years I've made a habit of cutting open the stomach and inspecting its contents. What I've found is that the striped bass regularly feeds on a wide variety of forage. Sometimes the stomach discloses only one type of forage, perhaps menhaden or sand eels. On other occasions I've found five or six different species, including squid, crabs, sand bugs, baby fluke, shrimp, and spearing, all packed tightly together. With lunker stripers, those over 30 pounds, I've observed upward of half a dozen adult mackerel, menhaden, and herring crammed side by side into the stomach; it made me wonder how it even got the last one in there!

If you're fishing from a boat, you should by all means always have ice in the fishbox. Shaved ice is best, and you should fill the stomach cavity with it, then bury the entire fish in ice; this will quickly lower the body temperature of the fish. Take care to ensure there is drainage from the fishbox—you want the melted ice water to drain off. Under no circumstances should the striper be submerged in water.

If you're fishing from the beach, where it's difficult to get back to the car, the best thing is to dig down into the sand around the high-water mark and bury the striper in the cool damp sand. This gets the fish out of the air and avoids the drying out that quickly happens when the heat of day and strong wind cause the fish to deteriorate.

Given current regulations that generally limit the catch of stripers, these preliminary steps take only a few minutes with the one or two fish that most anglers are apt to keep for the table. Believe me when I say the time expended is well worth it. You can defer the final cleaning until later.

The method you'll use for the final cleaning will depend on how the fish is to be prepared. Striped bass are often stuffed and baked whole, while some people prefer to steak larger striped bass, and fillets lend themselves to a wide variety of recipes.

Stripers that are to be served whole should first be scaled. If your fish have been properly cared for, and the skin has not been permitted to dry out, scaling will be relatively easy. Striped bass have large scales for their size, and it's best to use a sturdy scaler. Working in long strokes, draw the scaler from the tail of the fish toward the head. As long as the scales are moist, the scaler should easily remove them from the skin.

While many anglers use scissors to cut the fins from the fish, I strongly discourage this, for this leaves the root of the fins in the fish, which become those pesky little bones that are so bothersome as you eat fish. Instead, take a sharp knife and insert it alongside the dorsal fin, make a cut from the head of the fish toward the tail, and repeat on the other side of the dorsal fin. Then grasp the dorsal fin and remove it, roots and all, from the fish. Repeat this procedure with the anal fin, and then cut around and remove the caudal fins.

Some people prefer to bake their fish with the head intact. If this is the case, use a sharp knife to lift the gill cover and carefully cut away and discard the gills. If the head is to be removed, use a sharp knife and cut through at a slight angle just behind the gill covers. With big stripers it's difficult to cut through the thick backbone; after your knife has reached it, switch over to a serrated knife or a cutting saw to cut through it.

This leaves a scaled fish, with fins and head removed, and only the heavy backbone and rib cage bones, which are easily removed after the fish is cooked.

To prepare the fish for steaks, follow the procedure just outlined. Then simply slice off steaks to the desired thickness, with 1 inch being a popular, easy-to-cook size. Begin by cutting your steaks from the head and work toward the tail. As you reach the area of the anus, the tail section of the striper gets narrower, resulting in smaller steaks. Many anglers simply leave this section whole, completing the cleaning by cutting off the tail.

Filleting a striper is actually easier than preparing it whole or for steaks. A sharp filleting knife is the key. Begin by laying the fish flat on a cutting board, with its back facing you. Insert the knife into the back, alongside and ahead of the dorsal fin. About midway through the fish you'll feel resistance as the knife reaches the rib cage and backbone.

Begin cutting, moving from front to back along the backbone, working from the head toward the tail. As you approach the halfway mark in the length of the fish, you'll note that the rib cage ends, and you're able to push the knife all the way through the fish. Continue cutting, keeping the knife as near to the backbone as possible to avoid wasting any meat, until you finish the cut at the tail.

Go back to where you made your first incision. At an approximate 45-degree angle, make a cut from the top of the head, working the knife just behind the pectoral fin, and cutting down toward the stomach.

Again insert the knife in the initial cut—where you felt the pressure of the rib cage—and work the knife, cutting through the

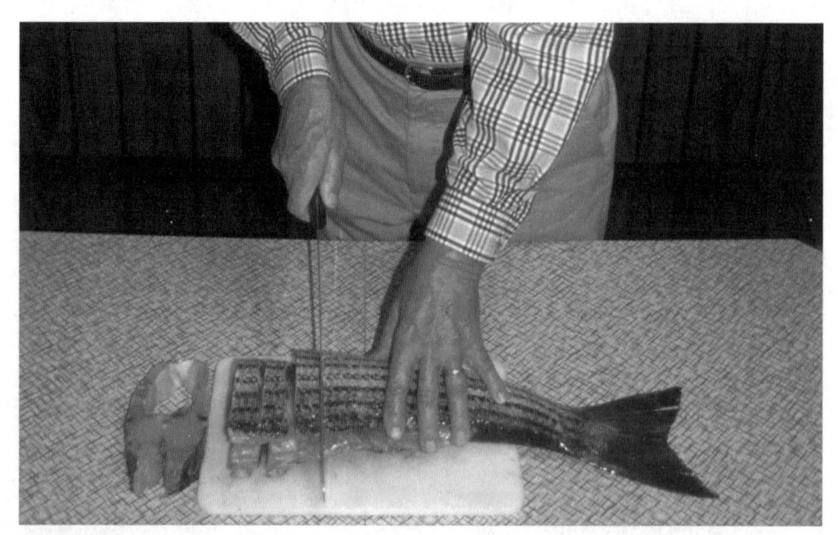

To prepare striped bass for steaking, use a scaler and work it from the tail to the head, removing all scales. Then cut along all the fins, removing them by their roots. The bass may then be cut into steaks, with ¾-inch to 1-inch-thick steaks preferred.

rib cage bones until you've cut through them all. In the case of striper weighing 15 pounds or more, it's sometimes easier to make this cut with a heavy, serrated cutting knife, which cuts through the bones easier. After this cut has been completed, place your knife into the stomach cavity and cut from the stomach toward where your knife cut through at the midsection of the fish, near the anal vent. Once you've cut through, you can lift off the slab of the entire side of the striper.

Now repeat this procedure on the other side of the fish, which leaves you with a second slab of fish, but not yet a fillet, as each piece still has the rib bones.

Lay each slab skin-side down and carefully work your knife from front to back between the meat and the rib bones, neatly cutting them away.

The next step is to begin at the tail, with the fillet resting on the skin, and work your knife between the skin and meat. Move the knife back and forth while holding on to the skin, so the sharp knife blade cuts between the skin and meat. The skin should come off easily, so long as you don't apply too much cutting pressure and cut through the skin.

The final step in cleaning is to remove the dark meat of the lateral line of the fish, which runs the length of the fish on the skin

The fillet in the foreground was cut from one side of the bass, and another fillet is being cut from the remaining side.

side of the fillet. Lay the fillet in front of you and make a neat cut at a 45-degree angle along the bottom of the lateral line. Make a second cut at the same angle along the top of the lateral line. This will enable you to neatly remove the entire strip of dark meat, which has a strong flavor; most people prefer not to eat it. This leaves you with a neat fillet, completely free of bones.

In the case of small stripers in the 3- to 5-pound class, the fillets are thin, and often prepared whole. With big stripers, however, especially those weighing 15 pounds or more, the fillets can take on monumental proportions. With really thick fillets, such as those measuring 3 inches or thicker, you can slice off portion-sized mini fillets, cutting much as you would a London broil.

You can also run your knife the length of the fish, cutting the fillets to a desired thickness, usually ¼ to ½ inch thick, and then cutting them a second time to the desired length, usually 8 to 10 inches, which are ideal serving size.

If you're fortunate to have made a good catch and have a surplus of striped bass, you're in luck, as they freeze extremely well. I've kept the white, firm meat frozen for up to two years, and when thawed and cooked it tasted like I'd caught it that afternoon. The key is not only proper handling when it's caught and subsequent cleaning, but how you freeze it.

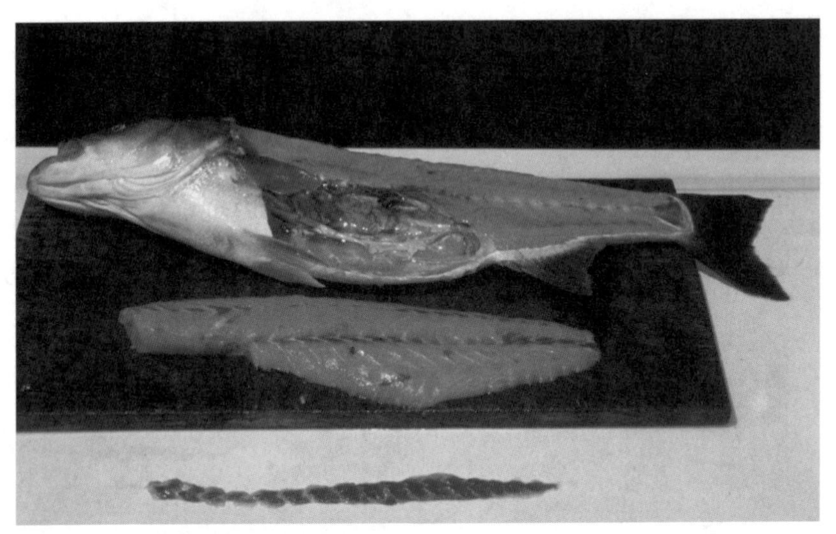

After cutting a fillet from each side of the striper, skin the fillet and then remove the dark strip of meat known as the lateral line. This dark meat has a very heavy flavor and should be discarded.

Don't even consider wrapping it in freezer paper, as was done years ago. It'll invariably get freezer burn, and after losing its moisture it will taste awful, and smell "fishy" as well.

I wouldn't pack it in plastic bags either; there's invariably some air in the bags, which in turn results in freezer burn.

Freezing the striper in plastic bags with the fish covered with water does a fairly good job of retaining its quality, but it's very space consuming and a nuisance to thaw. Resting too long in water during the thawing process doesn't help the flavor either.

The absolute best way to freeze stripers is to place them in packages of a size that you plan to use for a meal. Better to make many small packages than just a couple of large ones.

The key to successful freezing is vacuum-bagging. On the market today are small, countertop vacuum-bagging units that extract all of the air from each plastic package prior to freezing. For several years I've been using a food saver vacuum bagging system that has provided excellent results. This results in a neat package of fish that, when promptly frozen, lasts up to two years. When you've tried vacuum-bagging just once, you'll you become a believer. The frozen packages are just like the ones you may have seen in the supermarket, of fish such as tuna or swordfish that are frozen at sea. Once you've tried the vacuum-bagger with your freshly caught stripers you'll quickly be using it with other meats, vegetables, and fruits. For me it's a ritual to vacuum-freeze freshly picked and cooked Jersey corn during the summer, and enjoy it as a tasty treat during the height of winter.

My wife, June, will be sharing her favorite striped bass recipes with you in the next chapter. While these are her favorites, there are hundreds of more equally fine recipes out there, so don't hesitate to collect them as you go along. Once you've mastered the techniques of catching, caring for, and properly cleaning stripers, and then preparing them in the kitchen—we both share cooking those tasty bass at times—you'll get to enjoy what fresh fish should really taste like.

When the snow is fluttering down in midwinter, you'll be especially happy that there are a few packages of vacuum-bagged linesiders in the freezer!

CHAPTER 13

June's Favorite Striper Recipes

While catching a striped bass is a challenge and exciting, preparing your catch for dinner has equal appeal. When Milt and I married over 48 years ago, the very first fish I had to learn how to cook was striped bass!

I used the "normal" recipes—baking, broiling, and frying. But when Milt so frequently returned from his jetty haunts with school bass for the table, I found that the old recipes were somewhat tired. I began searching out and trying new ones. I also changed some of the old ones to suit our taste, and soon developed such a repertoire of recipes that for weeks at a time we'd seldom repeat one. Variety is the spice of life, they say, and by having a variety of striped bass recipes at your fingertips you'll really appreciate this fine game fish.

I leave the cleaning of striped bass to Milt, and he details exactly how to go about preparing the fish for the table in the previous chapter. This is extremely important, for the stripers we catch are properly cared for from the minute they're caught until they reach my kitchens. The recipes I'm including, as our favorites, are not the normal fry, broil, or bake variety. These require a bit more preparation time, but are certainly worth the effort, for the striper is an excellent table fish. It's white, firm, and has a texture that lends itself to preparing many ways.

So often people will read a recipe, and are hesitant about trying it. Don't fall into that pattern. Indeed, I'd ask you to promise that you'll try at least some of these recipes during the season ahead. By

Left: June Rosko shares her favorite striped bass recipes with you here, and she catches them as well, as evidenced by the beauty she's just beached not far from her home in Mantoloking, New Jersey.

all means don't hesitate to vary the recipes to suit your personal taste. A dash of cayenne here, added seasoning there, often makes a world of difference. Recipes evolve, and that's what makes cooking—and eating—so much fun.

Striped bass by itself, no matter the recipe, does not a meal make. Take care to plan and select fine vegetables to include with the recipes. Toward that end, I've mentioned the ones we enjoy, especially fresh from the garden or farm during peak season for the best choice. Just substitute those that spark your taste buds.

MACADAMIA NUT CRUSTED STRIPER

This is a favorite recipe of Gerry Gulli, executive chef of United Airlines, who originally prepared it for use with wahoo. Inasmuch as wahoo has the same white meat and firm texture as striped bass, I decided to try it, as I just love macadamia nuts. I was delighted with the results, and you will be, too. These proportions serve two people.

4 10-by-3-by-½-inch striped bass fillets (normally the fillets from a small bass are thick; they should be cut to size)

2 ounces finely chopped macadamia nuts

1 ounce seasoned bread crumbs

½ tablespoon toasted sesame seeds

½ teaspoon salt

½ teaspoon white pepper

2 ounces all-purpose flour

1 cup Eggbeaters (better for you, and the nuts stick better to Eggbeaters than to fresh eggs)

2 ounces olive oil

½ ounce clarified butter

Combine the macadamia nuts, bread crumbs, and sesame seeds, and lightly season with salt and pepper.

Dredge one side of a striper fillet in flour, and then dip the same side in the Eggbeaters. Dip the fillet into the macadamia nut mixture, pressing it firmly into the fish, so it sticks securely.

Heat the olive oil and butter blend in a saucepan for a couple of minutes, so it's very hot, but not burned. Sauté the striper with the crust side down until it takes on a golden-brown color, being careful not to burn it. Finish by turning it over to cook the other side, which is uncoated.

Test the fillet with a fork, and as soon as it flakes it's ready to serve. If you should choose to use thick fillets, up to 1 inch, you may finish them in the oven. Serve the striper with the crust side up.

I'll often use this recipe with the first striper of spring. At that time we've got fresh asparagus, and I'll mash some Yukon gold potatoes as a side dish. A light mushroom sauce over the fish makes for a striper seafood treat you'll long remember.

STRIPED BASS FRITTERS

I was introduced to conch fritters during our first visit to Bimini in the Bahamas some 40 years ago. They were a staple throughout the Bahamas. It wasn't until several years later that I discovered that you could make delicious fritters using scallops, shrimp, or firm white-meat fish like red snapper and grouper. The next natural extension was striped bass, with its firm-textured white meat.

4 striped bass fillets (approximately 10 ounces)
1 cup all-purpose flour
1½ teaspoons baking powder
1 egg
½ teaspoon salt
¼ teaspoon pepper
Dash of paprika
1 tablespoon pure canola oil
(has no cholesterol, and only 1 gram fat per serving)

Mix all of the ingredients, with the exception of the fish. Use an eggbeater or food processor to make a creamy batter. You can add beer or a nominal amount of milk to reach the right consistency.

Select a couple of fillets that would satisfy your appetite for dinner, and place them in a steamer. After just 4 minutes or so the fillets will be thoroughly steamed, and flake to the touch of a fork. Remove from the steamer and let cool. Then flake the fillets into pieces the size of a dime and add them to the batter, gently spooning them in, being careful not to crumble the fish.

Use a pitcher to pour the fish–batter mixture into a frying pan or pancake grill, much as you would do when making pancakes, and sauté until they take on a golden color. Serve them piping hot with a horseradish cocktail sauce or tartar sauce for a great treat. All you'll need is a nice tossed garden salad for a dinnertime treat that's really different.

STRIPED BASS ROCKEFELLER

Antoine Alciatore is said to have created an oyster dish in his New Orleans restaurant back in 1899, which a customer said was as "rich as Rockefeller." So came into being Oysters Rockefeller.

With so many seafood dishes it becomes the chef's choice as to how to proceed. Suffice to say that oysters aren't always available, so many folks tried other seafoods, including clams, scallops, and fillets of fish, with the striped bass a natural, as it has firm meat, not entirely unlike that of an oyster when cooked. I'll often add half a dozen sea scallops between the striped bass fillets, cutting the scallops in half so they're the same thickness as the fillets, which adds variety to a truly marvelous dish.

4 10-by-3-by-½-inch striped bass fillets
½ cup finely chopped scallions
½ cup finely chopped celery
2 tablespoons chopped parsley
1 10-ounce package frozen, chopped spinach
½ teaspoon Anisette
(has licorice flavor, if desired)
salt and pepper to taste
½ cup margarine
½ cup bread crumbs

Sauté the scallions, celery, and chopped parsley until they're tender. Add the mixture to a blender with the package of spinach,

Anisette, and salt and pepper to taste. Take care to blend until it takes on a pureelike consistency.

Lightly spray a Pyrex baking dish with Pam cooking spray, and add the four fillets side by side. Spoon the sauce on top.

Melt the margarine in a saucepan, taking care not to burn it. Then mix the melted margarine with the bread crumbs to a crumbly consistency and sprinkle on top of the spinach mixture.

Bake in a 450-degree oven for 8 to 10 minutes, until the fillets are done when they flake to the touch of a fork. Take care not to overcook.

I'll often put a couple of Idaho potatoes in the oven well before the fish. As soon as they feel like they're almost done, put the fish in the oven. The striper fillets, Rockefeller mixture, and baked potatoes with a dollop of sour cream always results in no leftovers.

BUD-BATTERED ROCKFISH

When Milt cleans a large rockfish, he'll make many nice, neat fillets, and often there are many small pieces from along the edges left over. I'll cut them into bite-sized pieces, and we'll have Bud-Battered Rockfish for dinner, a delicious change of pace. When a member of Anheuser-Busch's management team Milt always tried Budweiser beer in recipes, and this one's just great. You can, however, substitute skim milk for the Bud if you wish.

10 ounces rockfish (striped bass) fillet, in bite-sized pieces

1 lemon

4 heaping tablespoons all-purpose flour

salt and pepper to taste

1 package Eggbeaters (equivalent of 2 whole eggs)

½ teaspoon granulated sugar

8 dashes Worcestershire sauce

½ cup Budweiser beer (or skim milk),
to provide heavy consistency to the batter

Canola cooking oil

Squeeze the juice of the lemon onto the rockfish. Dredge the rockfish pieces in flour, salt, and pepper.

Mix all of the remaining ingredients, with the exception of the rockfish pieces and oil, and use an electric mixer to beat until the batter takes on a creamy consistency.

Place the batter mixture in the refrigerator for 2 hours to set, removing it half an hour before you plan to cook.

Use sufficient canola cooking oil in a frying pan so the bite-sized pieces will be not quite covered. Place the frying pan over moderate heat while you're battering the fish, so it is hot when you drop the battered rockfish pieces into it.

Dip the pieces, which many call fingers, in the creamy batter, so they're thoroughly covered.

Drop the pieces into the oil and they'll begin sizzling, which will trap the rockfish's flavor and juices within the batter. They'll fry quickly, with just a couple of minutes on each side all that is necessary to take on a golden-brown color. If you like fish extra crunchy, you can fry them a little longer without fear of them drying out. The crust will just be a little darker, and crunchy.

Place the Bud-Battered Fingers on paper toweling as you remove them from the frying pan.

They're perfect with tartar sauce or cocktail sauce dressing. Serve with french fries, garden-fresh string beans, and a lettuce and tomato salad, and clean plates will be the result.

ROCKFISH WITH HORSERADISH SAUCE

If you like horseradish, have I got a recipe for you! This one originated from Greg Zaczek, who sent it to Pete Barrett, editor of *The Fisherman*, who modified it, and we tried it, and I modified it. Here's my version, with the horseradish sauce just right for our taste.

4 thin-sliced rockfish fillets (¼ to ½ inch thick), weighing 1 pound

½ cup mayonnaise

2 tablespoons mustard

1 tablespoon freshly grated horseradish

Grated Parmesan cheese to cover fillets

Mix the mayonnaise, mustard, and horseradish to a creamy consistency.

Lightly coat the bottom of a Pyrex baking pan with Pam cooking spray. Place the four fillets in the pan. Completely cover the fillets with the mayo/mustard/horseradish mixture.

Lightly sprinkle grated Parmesan cheese over the mixture. Sprinkle heavily if you're a cheese lover.

Bake in a preheated 350-degree oven for 10 minutes, then move them to the broiler for about 5 minutes, or until the Parmesan takes on a golden-brown color and begins to bubble. By this time the rockfish should be done, but check it with a fork to make certain it flakes easily.

Serve this delightful rockfish dish with a tossed salad, with vinegar and oil dressing. If it's summertime, serve with corn on the cob.

That's all you'll need.

BIG AL WUTKOWSKI'S STRIPER FISHCAKES

Al Wutkowski's a big guy who likes to catch big stripers, and he's just about the best live-bait fisherman on the Atlantic coast. He regularly catches many lunkers from his boat *The Flume.* He likes to eat big, too, and many years ago shared his striper fishcake recipe with us. I take no credit for it, but at its conclusion will add a twist of my own.

2 pounds striped bass fillets
1 cup chopped Vidalia onions
1 cup chopped green or red bell peppers
1 cup whole-kernel corn
2 tablespoons virgin olive oil
2 tablespoons mayonnaise
1 tablespoon Dijon mustard
1 package Eggbeaters (equivalent of 2 whole eggs)
Old Bay Seasoning and hot red pepper flakes to taste
2 cups seasoned bread crumbs
Canola oil for frying

Cut the fillets into 3- or 4-inch cubes. Then steam or poach them for 8 to 10 minutes, or until the meat flakes at the touch of a fork.

Drain the fillet cubes in a colander, pressing out as much water as you can, so the delicate meat is nearly dry.

In small frying pan, sauté the onions, peppers, and corn in the olive oil until the onions have caramelized—turning a rich golden color—and the vegetables are tender. Remove the pan from the heat and set aside for later use.

In a large mixing bowl, mix the mayonnaise, mustard, Egg-beaters, and sautéed vegetables. If you like your fish cakes spicy, now's the time to add Old Bay Seasoning and red pepper flakes, to suit your taste.

Finally, add the fish and mix with your hands until the fish flakes into small pieces the size of crabmeat chunks. Add the seasoned bread crumbs, with just enough to hold the mixture together, making it easy to form into fishcakes.

You can make fishcakes of uniform size by using a ½- or ⅓-cup plastic measuring cup. Pack the mixture tightly into the cup. Hold the cup's handle and slap it hard, facedown, into the palm of your hand. This will pop the mixture out of the cup in a nicely formed fishcake of perfect size.

Place the canola oil in a frying pan and make certain it's sizzling. Add the fishcakes, using just enough oil in the pan so they're not covered. Fry the fish cakes until they're a golden brown. Always remember that it takes less time to fry the second side after you turn them over.

If you prefer not to fry, place the fishcakes on a cookie sheet sprayed with Pam cooking spray, and bake them in an oven at 350 degrees. It usually requires approximately 30 minutes to bake, or until they take on a golden-brown color.

When the fishcakes are removed from the frying pan or oven, place them on paper toweling and permit them to drain and cool. They take on a more delicate flavor after just 5 minutes of cooling. They're delicious when served with tartar sauce or a hot horseradish cocktail sauce.

When we make more fishcakes than we can use at one sitting, we vacuum-bag them and freeze them for future use.

Now I'll tell you my variation on this fine recipe. I use all the same ingredients, but in a different way, adding 2 medium-sized Yukon gold or Red Bliss potatoes. Remove the skins, boil the potatoes, and mash them. Where the recipe indicates adding the bread crumbs, add the mashed potatoes instead.

Continue to make the fishcakes as described earlier. Next, dip them in the bread crumbs, which will easily stick to the fishcakes; proceed to fry. The mashed potato results in a somewhat creamier fishcake, with the bread crumbs adding a crunchy exterior crust. They're just great eating, whether you stick with Big Al's original recipe and the fun variation I've created.

BAKED STRIPER IN WHITE ZINFANDEL

Baking is a wonderful way of cooking striped bass. Unfortunately, most of the baked striped bass that I've eaten while visiting friends or in restaurants has been dry and had a heavy flavor. This resulted from lack of moisture during cooking, resulting in a dry fish that often smelled "fishy." This recipe is pure delight, I assure you.

- 4 medium-sized striped bass fillets, not more than ½ inch thick
- 2 3-inch fresh tomatoes, sliced
- 1 tablespoon cornstarch
- 2 tablespoons margarine
- ½ cup skim milk
- ⅓ cup white Zinfandel
- ½ teaspoon fresh basil

Spray a pie-sized Pyrex baking dish with Pam cooking spray. Then place the fillets in the dish and cover with the sliced tomatoes.

In a small saucepan, melt the margarine over medium heat. Mix the tablespoon of cornstarch with ½ cup of water, as this will thicken the sauce, and not cause it to be lumpy, which is often the case with flour. Add this to the margarine, and gradually add skim milk until the sauce takes on a creamy or thick consistency—however you prefer. Remove the pan from the heat and gradually add the white Zinfandel and ½ teaspoon of fresh basil. (If you're concerned about the alcohol content, not to worry—it cooks away during baking.)

Pour the sauce over the fish and tomatoes and place in an oven that has been preheated to 350 degrees. Bake the dish for 25 to 30 minutes, until the striped bass flakes when tested with a fork.

I'll often prepare a potato casserole dish in the oven at the same time I'm preparing the fish. The striped bass, tomatoes, and potatoes, coupled with a garden-fresh salad of spinach, tomato slices, white mushroom buttons, and a Thousand Island dressing, has you on your way to a dinner you'll long remember.

STRIPED BASS AND APPLE STUFFING

This is a nice recipe for when there's a chill in the air, and just perfect for that last striper of the fall season, when you don't mind the oven heating up the kitchen.

- 1 3- to 6-pound whole striped bass, with scales, fin roots, and entrails removed
- 2 sliced Stayman Winesap apples, or a variety of your choice
- 1 sliced Bartlett pear, or a variety of your choice
- 1 packaged prepared poultry stuffing

Place the apple and pear slices in a steamer and precook them until you can stick a fork into them, but don't steam excessively so they fall apart.

While the apples and pear are steaming, follow the directions on the prepared poultry stuffing package, so it's ready to insert into the body cavity of the striper.

When the apples, pears, and stuffing are ready, use your hands to gently add in the apples and pear, so they're evenly distributed in the stuffing. Then use your hands to pack the stuffing mixture firmly into the body cavity. Some cooks like to tie the body cavity shut with light twine, but I opt to leave it open, as this results in the exposed stuffing getting nice and crunchy, much as when you're roasting a turkey.

I place a couple of dabs of margarine in the cavities that exist where the dorsal, pectoral, pelvic, and anal fins have been removed, as this keeps the exposed meat moist while baking.

Place the fish in a roasting pan, and, using a basting brush, baste the entire exterior with margarine, or spray it lightly with Pam cooking spray to keep it moist.

Preheat the oven to 350 degrees. The general rule of thumb is 8 to 12 minutes per pound. Keep in mind that ovens vary. My electric oven in Watchung cooks much quicker than the gas oven in Mantoloking. The key is periodically testing the fish. When the striper flakes easily when tested with a fork, and the exposed stuffing takes on a golden color and has formed a crunchy crust, it's time to serve.

I'll often include a halved butternut squash in the oven while the stuffed striper is baking. Brussels sprouts, broccoli, and cauliflower are at their peak during the fall, and they'll add to the dinner. The last cucumber of the season from the garden, its skin scored with a fork, then thinly sliced along with thinly sliced onions and served with a red wine vinaigrette dressing, combine as a tasty salad to result in a delicious seafood dinner.

STRIPED BASS FRANÇAISE

There aren't many seafood recipes that include garlic, but there are many garlic lovers out there like me, who just relish a dish whose flavor derives from these onionlike cloves. Française is so often associated with chicken and veal that few ever realize its potential with seafood—and with striped bass you've the perfect fish.

4–6 medium striped bass fillets, much the same quantity and thickness as if it were it veal cutlet

½ cup margarine (real chefs insist butter is better)

2–3 cloves garlic, depending on how much you like, although chopped garlic does just fine

½ lemon

½ cup white Zinfandel or Chardonnay

6–8 leaves of basil from the garden—
here, too, dried is fine

6 sprigs of parsley from the garden,
although dried is fine

½ container of Eggbeaters (equivalent to 1 fresh egg)

Begin by melting the margarine in a frying pan, over very low heat, taking care to keep it from burning.

Add the garlic and the juice of half a lemon, and continue cooking over moderate heat to release the garlic's flavor into the sauce.

Add the white Zinfandel, stirring it in, and then add the basil and parsley and turn down the heat to low, so it continues cooking but doesn't cook away.

Lightly salt and pepper the striper fillets and dip each in the Eggbeaters. Add them to the sauce and sauté for just a few minutes, then turn the fillets and continue cooking until they flake to the touch of a fork. Use a turnover and fork to remove the fillets from the sauce, as they'll easily fall apart if you're not careful. The beauty of this recipe is that the striper fillets are sautéing in sauce, which results in them not becoming dry and losing their flavor.

When you remove the fillets, you'll have some sauce remaining in the pan. It's good to add a little more white Zinfandel, and stir in a little cornstarch to thicken the sauce. Stir constantly, blend in all the accumulated pastelike, flavor-packed sauce in the pan, and serve in a small pitcher, to pour over the striper when you serve.

I'll often serve this dish with scalloped potatoes. A side dish of cubed yellow squash and zucchini is great. For a tasty salad, try cubed tomatoes with halved white button mushrooms and add a dash of balsamic vinegar. You'll have that urge to go out and catch another striper!

STRIPED BASS CHOWDER

When Milt wrote *Fishing the Big Four: Striper, Bluefish, Weakfish, and Fluke,* I included this recipe, and have received so many compliments that I'm including an expanded version here as well. Surprisingly, very few people have ever eaten fish chowder, and it's just delicious. While I've used it with many species, it originated with the striped bass.

Milt first enjoyed this recipe on a cold November morning while trolling for stripers aboard the *Linda June*. A friend had brought a thermos filled with the tasty chowder made from a bass caught the day before, and it's been a favorite ever since.

3 pounds striped bass fillets

4 large Vidalia onions, chopped

½ cup margarine

3 quarts water

10 medium-sized red new potatoes,
peeled and cut in ½-inch cubes

24 tiny carrots, peeled and cut in ½-inch pieces

4 cups milk

2 12-ounce cans evaporated milk

Sauté the chopped onions in the margarine in a large soup pot until caramelized and golden. Add the water, potatoes, and carrots, and set the range to a simmer. Once the carrots and potatoes feel tender to the fork, add the fish and continue on simmer. When the fish begins to flake, add the 4 cups of milk and the 2 cans of evaporated milk. Add salt and pepper to suit your taste. If you like a robust flavor, cayenne pepper or Old Bay Seasoning will do it.

With everything mixed together, stir lightly and continue to simmer until it is piping hot, but do not boil the chowder.

While I'm cooking, Milt repairs to Fumosa's Bakery in Ortley, New Jersey, for a loaf of their seeded rye bread. Fumosa's is an old-fashioned Italian bakery, and they bake the most delicious seeded rye you could ever imagine. It's a staple with striper chowder. You'll go back for seconds of the hearty chowder. It's so filling there's no need for a sandwich.

TERIYAKI GRILLED STRIPER

During the summer we do most of our cooking on the grill outdoors, but in the winter often use a countertop electric grill. Grilling is nice, for there are no pots to contend with. I've found that marinating striped bass for just 30 minutes gives it super taste when it's grilled, although some people prefer longer. Begin at 30 minutes and you can't go wrong.

4 striped bass steaks, weighing about ½ pound each

2 cups ginger-teriyaki or lemon-herb dressing marinade

Place the ginger-teriyaki or lemon-herb dressing in a Pyrex dish and marinate the steaks for just 30 minutes, as you don't want the marinate flavor to be overbearing.

Turn on your grill at least 15 minutes before you're ready to place the striper steaks on. You want the grill hot, so the sizzling heat seals the juices in the fish. Many people make the mistake of putting the fish on the grill, and then turning it on. As the grill is heating up, it is also drying out the fish, which makes it dry and chewy, and even causes it to smell "fishy."

Here again, timing is everything. Don't walk away and forget the fish. It normally takes but 3 or 4 minutes on each side, and you should baste with the marinade to keep the striper steaks moist while you're grilling.

I'll often make a tasty potato salad with small new potatoes, and serve a lettuce and tomato salad, resulting in a quick and easy dinner that we can enjoy out on the deck.

BLACKENED STRIPED BASS MAGIC

This recipe normally begins with redfish, which is really a channel bass, the meat of which is very similar to striped bass. What does blackened fish have to do with redfish? It's simply because Chef Paul Prudhomme began to use one of his magic seasoning blends with redfish. The rest is history, as blackened redfish became the rage, and Blackened Redfish Magic became the seasoning of choice with striped bass as well!

More years ago than I can remember Milt received a cast-iron skillet and country-cured bacon as a gift from a friend. The bacon was delicious and devoured. The cast-iron skillet remains, and has been used ever since as our utensil of choice for Blackened Striped Bass Magic, as I've come to call this recipe.

The smoke this recipe develops is overpowering, and it's best prepared outdoors, preferably over a hot grill. If blacken indoors you must, by all means turn on the exhaust fan early, and on high, and don't say I didn't warn you.

4 large striped bass steaks or fillets, ½ inch or thicker

½ cup margarine
(Chef Paul says use "unsalted butter")

1 shaker jar Chef Paul Prudhomme's Blackened
Redfish Magic

Pam cooking spray

Begin by placing a cast-iron skillet (a frying pan will do) on the grill or stove with medium heat at least 10 minutes before you plan to cook. You want the skillet sizzling hot.

Melt the margarine in a separate pan. Dip the striped bass fillets or steaks in the margarine, coating both sides well.

Sprinkle both sides of each steak or fillet with a liberal coating of Chef Paul's Blackened Redfish Magic seasoning. Raise the heat on the grill or stove and place the coated fish in the skillet. Be prepared to stand back, or become engulfed in smoke, as it happens quickly. Cook the bottom of the steak until it forms a sweet crust. Then turn and repeat. Take care not to cook excessively, as you don't want to dry the fish out. Test it with a fork; when it flakes to the touch, it's ready to serve. If you wish a sauce, melted margarine works just fine.

Be very careful when using a cast-iron skillet, as it gets extremely hot. Use a potholder at all times.

We'll often use this recipe during the summer, when most of our meals are prepared outdoors on the grill. It's the season of the year when fresh string beans, yellow squash, zucchini, sugar snap peas, white onions, and tiny potatoes can be combined and prepared in a wok for a perfect side dish. I'll often make coleslaw and sprinkle it with grated carrots for a salad that complements Blackened Striped Bass Magic.

STEAMED STRIPER AND CARAMELIZED VEGETABLES

Milt and I just love vegetables. There are so many varieties available and they're just delicious. The recipe included here is one that I never make twice using the same selection of vegetables. Whatever's available in the garden, or looks good in the produce department, gets brought into the mix.

The steaming of the striper is the easiest part, and requires just minutes. The caramelized vegetables result in a meal that's just delicious. I'll often get carried away with the vegetables and have leftovers that are delicious when served on a roll with hot dogs or sausages from the grill.

4 medium-sized striped bass fillets,
not over ½ inch thick

To steam fish you can use the same steam platform used to steam vegetables. Fill a large pot that will hold the steamer with approximately 1 inch of water. Bring the water to a boil, place your fillets on the steamer rack, and cover the pot. With the steam rising vigorously, carefully check the fillets with a fork periodically. The striper is finished when it flakes easily at the touch of a fork. Depending on the size and quantity of the fillets, this may only take 4 or 5 minutes.

Because caramelizing the vegetables takes so long, be prepared to steam the striper fillets once the vegetables are finished and waiting in the oven to be served.

1 2-by-8-inch eggplant

1 2-by-8-inch yellow squash or green zucchini

1 large green bell pepper

1 large red bell pepper

4 3-inch-diameter white mushrooms

2 3-inch-diameter Vidalia onions

6 3-inch-diameter ripe tomatoes

1–4 cloves of garlic crushed, or chopped garlic to taste

2 tablespoons virgin olive oil

Salt and pepper to taste

1 handful fresh basil or 1 tablespoon dry basil

Use a vegetable peeler to remove the skin from the eggplant, squash, and peppers. Cut all of the vegetables into ½-inch squares.

Place the vegetables into an 8-by-16-by-2-inch Pyrex baking dish. Sprinkle with the virgin olive oil and add a nominal amount of salt and pepper to taste. Finally, sprinkle with the basil, and use a large, long-handled cooking spoon to thoroughly mix all ingredients.

Preheat your oven to 525 degrees. That's right, 525 degrees! Then place the dish, the ingredients of which will have filled it to near overflowing, into the oven. It's important to check the baking vegetables at 5-minute intervals, carefully turning them frequently with a long-handled cooking spoon, so they will cook thoroughly, but not burn. After half an hour or thereabouts you'll notice that the vegetables have cooked down, with the dish appearing only half full, with quite a bit of juice in the bottom.

To finish the sauce, switch the oven from baking to broiling, and leave the oven door open. Continue stirring for 5 or 10 more minutes, until the vegetables are thoroughly caramelized, taking on a beautiful brown color and thickening as the liquid slowly disappears. If the liquid completely cooks away, and you wish to have the sauce take on a deeper color and richer flavor, stir in a nominal amount of water to keep it from burning, turning the vegetables all the time until they reach a consistency you desire.

Place the fish on a serving platter using a small turnover, as the steamed striper is very delicate and will fall apart easily. Because it's quite bland, most people will lightly salt and pepper the striper before pouring the piping-hot sauce over it. A salad of fresh cucumber and onions with an oil and vinegar dressing complements the meal nicely.

HICKORY-SMOKED STRIPER

Years ago whiting were very plentiful along the Middle Atlantic coast, and each fall, between Thanksgiving and Christmas, we'd catch a bunch. In those days we'd drop them off at LeRoy's Fishery in Atlantic Highlands, New Jersey, using a barter system. A week later we'd pick up half of the catch, delicately smoked, and LeRoy would retain the remainder for resale.

As a result of commercial exploitation, the whiting population virtually disappeared, and urban sprawl resulted in ordinances that prohibited smokehouses. To solve the smoking dilemma, our children gave us a Little Chief home electric smoker. We tried smoking mackerel for Christmas, and they were delicious, but the oily fish did not keep for more than a week.

Milt often caught the last school stripers from the beach early in December, and he experimented with smoking these. The firm, white meat of the bass is absolutely delicious when smoked. With school bass he'll take a fillet off each side, leaving the skin on. He'll then cut the fillet in half lengthwise, resulting in a second fillet. This will result in two fillets for the smoker with skin on, and two fillets without skin. We like this better than a thick fillet for smoking, as it enables me to cut ½-inch-thick slices for serving.

You'll require a Little Chief home electric smoker or comparable model for this recipe. As with most fish recipes, you can experiment and develop your own exotic brine and bring an entirely new taste to your smoked fish as a result. Here's how Milt does it.

4 16-by-4-by-½-inch striped bass fillets
(2 with skin, 2 without, from one small striper)

½ cup noniodized salt

½ cup white granulated sugar

1 package hickory or apple wood smoking chips

Smoking requires time and patience. As with good wine, it can't be rushed.

You'll require a brine solution. Mix ½ cup of noniodized salt and ½ cup of white sugar, and add this to a quart jar half filled with warm tap water. Place a cap on the jar and shake vigorously until the salt and sugar are dissolved. Complete filling the jar with water and again shake vigorously. Place the brine in the refrigerator to chill.

Place the fillets you plan to smoke in a glass or Pyrex baking dish—not metal—and pour in sufficient brine to cover the fish. Refrigerate overnight, or 8 to 12 hours, turning the fillets once or twice to ensure complete brining. Through experimentation you'll find just the right amount of brine time that suits your taste.

Next, remove the fish from the brine and pat each piece dry with paper toweling. Permit the pieces to air-dry for at least an hour, until the fish takes on a tacky glaze, called a pellicle.

Place your smoker outdoors, on the patio or in the driveway, on a day when there's no chance of rain. While the brined fish is air-drying, turn on your electric smoker and let it get piping hot, without any wood chips in the pan.

It's good to spray the smoker racks with Pam cooking spray, which keeps the fillets from sticking. Next, place the striper fillets to be smoked on the smoker's racks and insert them into the smoker.

Fill the smoker pan with hickory chips and insert it into the smoker. Within a few minutes you'll see that the heating element causes the wood chips to begin smoldering, giving off smoke, which will rise through the smoker and exit. There are a variety of wood chips available—apple, cherry, and others—and you can experiment to your heart's content until you achieve a flavor that suits your taste.

It will take half an hour or more for a pan of wood chips to completely smolder, turning black and no longer giving off any smoke. Remove the spent chips and add another pan of chips. For average-sized fillets from a small striper, two pans of hickory chips are usually sufficient and give a delicate smoked flavor in about an hour or two.

It is necessary to leave the fish in the smoker for a total of 6 to 8, or even 10, hours, to permit the heat of the smoker to dry the fish. Taste a small piece once it takes on that golden color, and adjust the smoking time and drying time to get just the right flavor.

Some people so enjoy smoked fish that they make a meal of it. It's especially nice when placed on a bed of Boston lettuce on a dinner plate, encircled with cubed cucumbers, mushrooms, peppers, scallions, and radishes. Just a touch of fat-free Russian or French dressing and you'll be glad you invested the time and effort to smoke your catch.

Smoked striped bass is also a welcome treat for the holidays. It's our replacement for whiting, and a delicious one at that. Use a very sharp filleting knife to slice the fillets into thin strips, and serve on thin crackers.

Bon Appétit!

At this juncture I've lost count of the locations where we've caught stripers while traveling along the seacoast and to inland impoundments and rivers. It's been fun, and along the way we've had our stripers prepared many ways.

I've included here those recipes that are different, and which we've enjoyed the most and felt would pique your interest. If you've read this far, you'll recall earlier I asked that you promise to try at least some of these recipes in the season ahead. If you're a seafood lover, you'll try them all . . . and I'm certain you won't regret having prepared a single one!

CHAPTER 14

Finding the Elusive Striper

In a book such as this it would be virtually impossible to go into great detail regarding specific spots and locations where striped bass are caught. I've chosen instead to include all of the coastal states and will highlight the primary striped bass fishing areas and the most popular techniques that are employed in them.

It is important to note that striped bass have been introduced and now reproduce in the fresh waters of more than 20 inland states. The similarities of Lakes Marion and Moultrie in South Carolina, and Lake Texoma in Texas and Oklahoma are such that the techniques used in these impoundments are equally effective throughout the fresh waters where stripers now reside and reproduce.

Much the same can be said of the population of striped bass that has extended its range to include the Canadian Maritime provinces. Many stripers expand their range into these far north waters for short periods of time, which vary from season to season, most often dependent upon availability of forage. The techniques employed throughout the primary range of stripers produce equally good results for linesiders that have strayed over the border into Canadian waters.

Left: Claud Bain unhooks a striped bass just netted by Captain Jim Wright of the Therapy. *He hooked it on the broad expanse of the Chesapeake Bay while sailing from Virginia Beach. The bay is the major spawning area for Atlantic coast stripers and provides a wide variety of angling opportunities.*

ALABAMA

Alabama enjoys only about 60 miles of coast on the Gulf of Mexico. Mobile Bay constitutes much of its coastline, with several major river systems, including the Tombigbee and Alabama Rivers. The Tallapoosa and Coosa Rivers feed into the Alabama north of Montgomery. Many stripers travel over 300 miles through the various watersheds of the state and provide fine fishing.

Many of the state's impoundments also have substantial populations of striped bass, making them one of the largest game fish caught in Alabama's in inland waters.

While the striped bass population travels great distances inland, few stripers ever move into the Gulf of Mexico to migrate, nor are they fished for from the nominal surf along Alabama's limited shoreline.

CALIFORNIA

Along the northern New Jersey coast, the Navesink River empties into the Shrewsbury, which in turn empties into the broad expanse of Sandy Hook Bay. Back in 1879 and 1881 a pioneer fish culturist named Livingston Stone netted fewer than 500 striped bass in the Navesink River and transported them via railroad car to the Pacific coast. They were fingerlings measuring just 1½ to 3 inches in length, and were stocked in the broad expanse of San Francisco Bay. Little did anyone realize how well the striper would adapt to its new home waters, which were not unlike those of many Atlantic coast bays and rivers. Today they are considered a major game fish in their adopted waters, providing California and Oregon anglers with fine sport, thanks in great part to sound fisheries management.

Back in the mid-1960s I was pondering writing a book on striped bass, but one of the few places I had never fished for them was in California. I'd often thought about those California fish that were close cousins of the first striper I caught in the Shrewsbury River, just a couple of miles from where the transplanted fish were netted many years earlier.

Having learned that the best way to succeed when seeking stripers is to team up with a veteran angler, I called two well-known striper angler-writers before my first trek west. The first call was to Leon Adams, author of *Striped Bass Fishing in California and Oregon.* The second call was to Larry Green, who not only was a superb writer and excellent striped bass angler, but also a pioneer in West Coast fly fishing for stripers. The dates were set, and my rod case was packed with a popping outfit and 9-weight fly rod and floating line.

Leon was executive director of the California Wine Institute, and on boarding his 18-foot Lyman, he passed aboard lunch in a wicker basket containing French bread, cheese and a couple of bottles of Barbera, a wine I'd never heard of. Coming from a brewing background at Anheuser-Busch, my standard fare was a cold Bud and roast beef sandwich when we fished East Coast striper haunts. But, as the saying goes, "when in Rome." I've enjoyed fine California Barbera wine ever since!

Our first stop was at a bait receiver, where we took aboard a single scoop—large net full—of live anchovies and shiners, as insurance in the event we failed to score on artificials. The tide was roaring out of San Francisco Bay as we approached the South Tower of the Golden Gate Bridge. Leon instructed Emil, his brother, and me to cast from the bow toward the tower, while he stemmed the swift current. It took me just two casts with an Upperman Bucktail jig to hook up. No more than 20 casts later we'd each landed our limit of three stripers, with fish ranging from 5 to 21 pounds.

Years later, when the Verrazano Narrows Bridge was built in New York, I employed Leon's exact same techniques on my first visit to the bridge's East Tower, and enjoyed a repeat performance. I make mention of this outing to emphasize the importance of having a wide range of techniques and tackle at your disposal. Knowledge and experience enable you to maximize your enjoyment, no matter the location.

As with striper populations on the East Coast, the Pacific stripers have gone through cycles when stocks were depleted, but through sound management practices and improved water quality California anglers today enjoy excellent fishing. While stripers are regularly caught in the open reaches of the Pacific, the bulk of the population remains in bay waters throughout their life cycle. As with East Coast populations, several distinct strains have developed, each returning to its home waters to spawn during the spring.

The San Francisco Bay and San Pablo Bay hold by far the largest concentrations, with the majority of fish caught from small boats. A sizable fleet of party boat and charter boats regularly scores with the plentiful bass. Live bait such as anchovies, shiners, sardines, and other forage species are fished in the many rips, and along channel edges and ledges where bass congregate to feed on forage carried by the current. On my very first visit to Raccoon Straits a live anchovy was nailed while drifting it along the bottom. It was the first of many bass caught on this popular baitfish throughout San Francisco Bay and San Pablo Bay.

Both of these bays are fed by an extensive river system pouring in from the mountains to the east. They include the Sacramento and San Joaquin Rivers, which, along with the Suisan and Grizzly Bay, not only provide fine fishing for stripers but serve as a spawning and nursery area as well, with the fish moving fully 20 miles upriver to spawn and feed on the abundant smelt during spring.

As I fished many areas of the bays and the river systems that flow into them, I was reminded of waters of the Chesapeake Bay. While much of the region is densely populated, there are areas of picturesque shoreline and marsh. The stripers adapt well, and anglers are able to fish for them using a wide variety of techniques.

When Larry Green and I sat down in his living room, our children joined theirs and the wives gathered to share their traveling and fishing experiences. Larry and I talked flies. At the time his

Fog settles in from the Pacific Ocean as a striped bass is brought aboard from the waters of San Francisco Bay, not far from the Golden Gate Bridge. The bass inhaled a live anchovy bait drifted through the swirling tide rips on an ebbing tide.

West Coast patterns differed from the Joe Brooks's Blonde series that I'd had such great success with back home, along with cork-bodied poppers.

On the water I learned that I should have brought a sinking line, as Larry liked a line that got the fly down quick. At the time the sinking fly lines we used sank in slow motion, and couldn't begin to compare to the 400-plus-grain lines available to today's fly casters. Still, the floating line was perfect along the marsh grass when casting poppers and Honey Blonde and Platinum Blonde patterns tight to the bank.

Utopia was to locate small schools of stripers chasing bait on top, with birds working. Both the fly rod and casting rod provided sterling sport with 3- to 8-pound linesiders that were so fat their stomachs bulged.

Surf fishing the California beaches is unlike what I was accustomed to back east. It's awesome looking over your shoulder at majestic mountains as you prepare to cast. The sand is dark, unlike the near-white sand of some of our Atlantic beaches. The waves were often awesome. It's big-rod country to be sure, where heavy metal squids and leadhead jigs are the favorites of beach casters. Bottom rigs with natural chunk baits account for many stripers each season, with herring, anchovies, and sardines favored.

While I've experimented with teasers from Pacific beaches, I never spent sufficient time there to render a judgment as to their effectiveness. I suspect that if Pacific beach casters—as well as those who cast or jig other artificials from boats—were to religiously use a teaser such as a chartreuse-and-white with silver Mylar saltwater Clouser Minnow on a 3/0 hook, they'd be surprised at the results by season's end.

CONNECTICUT

George Seemann's home in Wilson Point, Connecticut, overlooked the broad expanse of Long Island Sound. George was an old friend, and captain of the *Mitchell II*, with whom June and I had fished with in many of the world's exotic angling playgrounds, and he loved to fish his home waters.

So it was with but a single toss of his cast net that he engulfed a huge school of 4-inch-long peanut bunker, fry of the year. The two of us struggled to lift the net, filled with tiny fry, aboard his

Boston Whaler. We quickly topped off a 5-gallon pail, added a couple of dozen to his live well, and promptly released the rest.

Such was my introduction to fishing with live menhaden in the fertile waters of Connecticut. George anchored up and chummed with small chunks of the bunker. He chummed sparingly; he didn't want to feed the stripers, just attract them. We then livelined the tiny bunker back in the chum line . . . and you know the rest of the story!

Connecticut has close to 100 miles of shoreline along Long Island Sound that provides every type of striped bass fishing you could ask for. There's boat fishing in the open sound, where small-boat, charter, and party boat anglers catch stripers trolling, fishing live bait, jigging, and casting.

Miles of beach and myriad groins, jetties, and rock piles encompass the coastline, all favorite haunts of stripers searching for a meal. There are protected waterways, too, at Greenwich, Stamford, Norwalk, Bridgeport, Stratford, Niantic, Waterford, Groton, and New London, to mention but a few of the most popular locations. While charter and party boats sail from the abundant marinas in these communities, often you can catch stripers right in the protected harbors.

In recent years fly fishing for stripers has grown in popularity, among both shore-based anglers and those fishing from shallow-draft flats boats. The great majority of stripers caught in sound waters are Hudson River stock, which begin arriving in late March and stay until year's end. Some even spend the winter, especially around the warm-water discharges of the generating plants located along the shoreline. Thus, you're often able to catch school stripers while plugging or casting a leadhead during the height of a snowstorm in January!

DELAWARE

The inlet at Indian River is typical of many found along the Middle Atlantic coast. A pair of rock jetties that extend seaward help protect the inlet from excessive shoaling. I've fished these jetties on many occasions, enjoying stripers that succumbed to the inlet jetty techniques discussed elsewhere in this book. The spot's a natural, for on an ebbing tide huge quantities of grass shrimp, crabs, and forage species are carried seaward, where stripers take up station in the rips and eddies to feed. If you visit Delaware, the inlet's a must.

Delaware has a beautiful seacoast, ranging from Cape Henlopen to Bethany Beach, with easy access and fine surf sport, particularly as the spring and fall migrations from the Chesapeake move through.

The state has two barrier beach bays, Rehoboth Bay and Indian River Bay, both of which are shallow and have healthy populations of "rockfish," as the natives call the striper. This is light-tackle fishing from a small boat at its finest, with small plugs and plastic-tailed leadhead jigs the favorite lures.

If you like to fish live bait, the spot, popularly called Lafayette, is very plentiful and is without question the favorite, with eels a close second. They may be caught from almost any dock or bulkhead using a size 8 or 9 Claw-style hook and piece of clam or sandworm bait.

Lewes is the kick-off spot for the broad expanse of lower Delaware Bay. A fine fleet of charter and party boats is available, with many specializing in stripers during the height of the spring and fall runs. This huge expanse of water, fed by the Delaware River—which pours 13 billion gallons of fresh water into it daily—teems with striped bass. It has been said that during severe drought conditions, each days sees fully 1,000 billion gallons of salt water enter the river, actually resulting in brackish water being found as far north as Philadelphia, fully 100 miles away.

Stripers have adapted well to this mixture, and many gradually leave the salt and, move up the Delaware River, where they feed extensively on herring and shad fry, and much to the chagrin of anglers, consume many trout, smallmouth bass, walleyes, and other game fish.

Throughout Delaware Bay, and the Delaware River that snakes its way north, the majority of fishing is done from small boats. Casting with artificials is popular, although many seasoned anglers probe these waters with live baits and consistently post fine scores, with many large stripers landed each season.

FLORIDA

Every book and research paper I've ever read about striped bass say unequivocally that striped bass are found throughout many of Florida's river systems. There appear to be two distinct groups of bass. One inhabits the rivers of northeast Florida, including the St. Johns, which has the largest striper population, and the St. Marys and Nassau Rivers. The Gulf coast populations of stripers, on the other hand, inhabit the many rivers that empty into the Gulf of Mexico, including the Ochlockonee, Apalachicola, Chociawhatchee, and Yellow Rivers, to name but a few of the major waterways.

I've often fished expressly for stripers in many of these waterways on both the Atlantic and Gulf coasts, but I've never landed a striper from Florida waters. I caught largemouth bass on plugs and spinnerbaits, catfish on live shiners intended for stripers, but old linesides has eluded me. I did learn, however, that these are distinct populations that are seldom, if ever, found in the open reaches of the Atlantic Ocean, or Gulf of Mexico.

The techniques used by the many guides and friends I've fished with parallel those used in the many bays and rivers of the Northeast. One-handed spinning or light bait-casting tackle is favored. Popping plugs, surface swimmers, and darters find favor, and rattle plugs have become a favorite of Florida striper anglers in recent years. The large Florida shiner has long been a favorite of bait fishermen, who ply the slow-running rivers while either anchored or drifting through the known striper haunts.

Both large and grass shrimp are found in the many waters frequented by striped bass. Florida anglers frequently use a single live shrimp as bait while fishing the slow-moving rivers located in the northeast section of the state.

GEORGIA

The coastal plain of Georgia is flat and covered with marshes and wetlands, with a variety of river systems slowly meandering their way to the ocean, the largest of which is the Savannah. Just a short distance off the coast are the Sea Islands, a vast collection of islands of assorted size, some inhabited, some not. The majority of the rivers that flow to the sea support a population of striped bass. The state's many impoundments also provide spectacular striper fishing despite being hundreds of miles from the sea.

My first visit to the Savannah River many years ago resulted in my catching striped bass, channel bass, and sea trout on the same outing while fishing with renowned outdoor scribe George Reiger. The favored technique was to anchor along the riverbank and fish with live shrimp, suspended 5 feet beneath a large popping float. What that inaugural trip taught me was that the fish moved great distances during the course of a tide, searching for forage. There would be spurts of action as the fish moved through, sometimes all three species intermingled and feeding together. The water in this river is often so turbid that you wonder how the fish can even see.

Georgia has hundreds of miles of picturesque creeks that meander through the marshes along the seacoast. Stripers populate many of them, providing exciting casting opportunities in a idyllic setting.

Subsequent trips expanded the techniques I employed, with several nice school stripers taken on bucktail jigs with a strip of pork rind cast along the riverbank, or to schools that were chasing bait on the surface. Fishing the marsh creeks and estuaries along the coast offers great opportunities for the fly caster.

This is primarily small-boat fishing country, with myriad creeks meandering through the marshes and ultimately emptying into the Altamaha, Ogeechee, Wilmington, Medway, and other rivers. The creeks and rivers in many places are very deep, with substantial tidal flow and a great abundance of forage, including the young of many species and shrimp. It's beautiful country to fish, ideally suited to one-handed spinning, a popping outfit, or fly casting along the marsh banks.

Many of the populations of stripers found in these rivers spend the summers in the lower reaches, moving up into brackish waters to spend the winter and eventually spawn. It doesn't appear there is the migration movement associated with populations such as those from the Hudson River and Chesapeake Bay to the north.

Georgia does not have the typical ocean fishery for stripers that anglers to the north are accustomed to.

LOUISIANA

Several river systems that form part of the Mississippi Delta for many years held populations of stripers that spent their entire life within their respective rivers. During recent years a phenomenon, attributed to nutrients inadvertently entering the Mississippi River drainage as a result of fertilizers used in agriculture, has greatly devastated, if not completely eliminated the tiny fishery that once existed.

To add to the state's difficulty, for several years during which there was a drought through the lower Mississippi they experienced record-setting salinity levels, which caused entire populations of inshore species, including the nominal population of striped bass, to vacate their favorite haunts. Many species, no doubt including the striped bass, moved into open Gulf waters, as salinity reached 30 parts per 1,000 and sea-surface temperatures reached the mid-80s. As a result of excess nutrients and abnormally high salinity, there was substantial attrition of the striped bass population.

The Louisiana Department of Fish and Wildlife has attempted to reintroduce the striped bass into the Tchefuncte and Bogue Falaya near Covington. Two different Gulf strains of striped bass fingerlings are being stocked, from which biologists can later determine which group had the best survival rate, and will serve as the basis for future stocking.

MAINE

My son Bob was just four years old when he and seven-year-old Linda caught their first stripers. The spot was the picturesque Saco River, which teemed with school stripers as we sailed from the cozy community of Biddeford. Trolling from a small outboard boat of Bob Boilard, we used soft plastic eels 6 to 8 inches in length, and added a sandworm, the latter resulting in more strikes than the plastic eel alone.

I spent a long time trying before I landed my first striper many years earlier, but on this occasion the bass were so plentiful and cooperative I could hardly believe it, as we landed several dozen during the day, with Linda and Bob having a ball. As the children tired June and I even got to fish, using light popping outfits, which maximized the sport.

I was soon to learn that Maine supported a sizable population of stripers throughout its many river systems and expansive bays. Bass move along the ocean beaches, too. Where I had been accustomed to fishing Jersey beaches wearing only a bathing suit, I soon found the Maine surf sport required waders—even in midsummer there's a chill to the water, make no mistake about it. I also learned that the rise and fall of the tide in Maine is extraordinary, with 12- to 20-foot tides as you move north. Entire rivers seem to simply disappear on the ebb, with extremely fast currents playing a role when you plan a strategy to fish them.

Maine has literally dozens of rivers, many of which empty into picturesque bays. While traveling the coast in a pickup camper and a motor home, we enjoyed superb striper fishing at almost all the locales we visited. Maine has an abundance of campgrounds along the coast, where you can really commune with nature. At many locales our campsite overlooked the waters we later fished, and often we'd lie in our bunks and hear the bells of the sea buoys, so close to the water were we. Boothbay Harbor comes to mind as a locale where the entire family enjoyed not only the fishing, but also many a lobster feast. The scenery, especially at the river mouths and the bays, many of which are dotted with small islands, is breathtaking, with magnificent woodlands and rocky promontories, sheer cliffs, and waters with a healthy population of stripers.

Among the rivers that provide sterling action are the York, Scarborough, Kennebec, Damariscotta, and Union, to mention but a few. The adjoining bays also provided us fine sport, as was the case in Penobscot, Casco, Sheepscot, and Frenchman Bays. I suspect you could spend a lifetime and never get to fish all of the bays and rivers of Maine along its over 200 miles of magnificent coast.

By all means fish with light tackle; a one-handed spinning or popping outfit, and an 8- or 9-weight fly-casting outfit is ideal, as many of the fish range from 4 to 10 pounds. Sandworms are easily obtained throughout Maine, which is where most are dug commercially to supply the entire East Coast. They're a favorite of bait fishermen, although small herring and mackerel also account for many linesiders each season.

If you're casting with artificials, use small swimming plugs, rattle plugs, poppers, and mirror plugs. I've also scored well with

This picturesque campsite overlooks the Maine coastline; in the waters below, striped bass are taken throughout the summer months. It's a great opportunity to combine family fun and fishing enjoyment along a beautiful section of seacoast.

leadhead jigs, with either bucktail or soft plastic skirts. Because I was often unfamiliar with the waters I was fishing, I'd troll the river systems and bays. Once I located fish, often with the help of gulls and terns working bait, I'd shut down the outboard and break out casting tackle. Often I was fooled, and the surface action resulted in harbor pollack and mackerel on the lures intended for stripers.

The range of the striped bass results in so many contrasts—from the broad, flat salt marshes of Georgia to Maine's rocky coastline—that it adds to the excitement that makes me long for more time to enjoy this contemplative pastime.

MARYLAND

I was introduced to the Chesapeake Bay, its "rockfish" population and chumming with grass shrimp on a pleasant day in the late 1940s. The place was Rock Hall, Maryland, a cozy community hard on the banks of the enormous bay.

I also learned quickly of the habits of schools of stripers congregating wherever a food source existed. In this case it was a rip line formed well off from a point of land, where currents collided with a shallow ledge extending up from the bottom. The skipper I sailed with didn't have the spot to himself, and I was surprised when fully five charter boats anchored and rafted up, tied side by side. With four or five anglers per boat, it was party time, and once everybody was in place, chumming with grass shrimp began.

We used freshwater bait-casting outfits, with short, 4-foot-long rods. This enabled you to reach up, grasp the line, and pull 3- to 4-foot-long lengths of line from the reel. The line was Cuttyhunk linen, with a 3-foot-long piece of "cat gut leader," as it was called in those days, and a 2/0 Sproat-style hook.

The captains chummed ever so sparingly, each dispensing just half a dozen shrimp at a time, which were quickly carried off with the current.

I was instructed to give 8 to 10 pulls of line and let it drift out into the current. I hadn't even made three pulls when an angler on an adjoining boat let out a whoop, his light rod buckled over with a striper. From that beginning, there were times when 10 anglers were simultaneously fighting school stripers from the five rafted-up boats.

At first the stripers held well back in the chum line, and occasionally strikes would be received with 12 or 14 pulls of line, equating to 48 to 56 feet of linen. Eventually they began to vie for the chum, and with as few as six or eight pulls of line we'd be into fish.

With the tide boiling, the action was fast and furious. As the tide slowed, the rip line began to dissipate, and as quickly as the action began, it stopped. It didn't slow down, it just stopped, as the fish moved off en masse to take up station in another rip, or to roam the Chesapeake searching for another meal.

There are a thousand stories like this that could be told about sport fishing for stripers in Maryland, for the state has a huge shoreline fronting the upper reaches of the Chesapeake Bay.

The variety of fishing in the waters of the bay and the multitude of rivers that empty into it defy description. I've scored on the Susquehanna flats, catching stripers quite by accident on shad darts while fishing for American shad during the spring run just off from Havre de Grace.

While I haven't fished all of them, the Northeast, Elk, Bush, Gunpowder, Patapso, Magothy, and Chester Rivers all produce bass. The rivers are populated primarily by pan-sized rock, and provide

During the spring a large fleet of boats congregates at the mouth of the Susquehanna River, where it empties into the upper reaches of the Chesapeake Bay. Here Maryland anglers score with migrating striped bass, plus herring and shad.

fine sport for fly fishermen as well as casters employing poppers, swimmers, and leadhead jigs. You can anchor up and chum effectively, too, and while years ago grass shrimp was favored, today sees increased use of chunks of bunker and clam bellies, as they're easier to obtain and less costly than grass shrimp.

Not to be overlooked is the open expanse of bay itself, where trolling is by far the most consistent method of catching rockfish. I've enjoyed superb sport off Chesapeake Beach while trolling for big bass. Spoons, swimming plugs, tube lures, and umbrella rigs sent into the depths on wire line consistently take the larger fish.

It always pays to have casting tackle rigged and ready, because often the bay will erupt as school stripers chase bait to the surface, with the accompanying canopy of birds working the bait as well. I've regularly experienced exciting surface action while fishing out of Crisfield, and also off Smith and Tangier Islands in midbay. This is big, open water, and it can get very mean with strong winds, creating heavy seas not unlike the open ocean. Always take care if you venture forth in a small boat, and check weather reports before departure. It can get nasty very quickly.

There are thousands upon thousands of docks, bridges, breakwaters, and bulkheads throughout Maryland's myriad waterways, and most of them at one time or another provide a casting platform from which to catch stripers, as do the miles of bay and river shoreline. The techniques discussed in the chapter devoted to docks and bridges will ensure fine catches from these waters.

MASSACHUSETTS

Mention Massachusetts and Cape Cod immediately comes to mind. I was introduced to the state's exciting striped bass fishing on the outer Cape. Frank Woolner, my writing mentor and editor of *Salt Water Sportsman,* invited the family to visit. Frank was a Cape Cod striper regular who lived in Worcester when he wasn't living in his beach buggy parked on the beautiful sand beaches.

Frank was a surfman of the first order and a gentleman second to none. He was also a tin-boat fanatic who liked to launch from the beach, which we did the day we arrived. In Jersey our water never had the clarity that I found on the Cape. As Frank motored to his favorite haunts we quickly found gulls working, and water that was air-clear. You could see the stripers chasing bait and literally sight cast swimming and popping plugs to feeding fish. See a fish, cast to it, and hold on as an eruption occurred!

To this day there's excellent striper fishing throughout the state. The outer Cape's beaches are a surf caster's delight, ranging from Race Point to Chatham, a distance of over 30 miles of beautiful sand beaches. All the techniques described earlier for use from the surf, with both lures and natural baits, work ideally from these beaches. Cape Codders like the long 10- to 12-foot surf rods, as with an onshore wind they like to be able to punch out long casts. Ask a Cape Cod regular of his choice of lures; "Surface-swimming plug, with a teaser rigged ahead of it" will be an instant response. As to natural baits, a live eel cast from the beach on a summer or fall night has little chance of survival.

Not to be overlooked is the lengthy coastline between the outer Cape and Cape Ann, where beach-based anglers and jetty jockeys regularly post scores with big stripers. If you're a visitor to this beautiful section of coastline, use the same surf and jetty techniques you're accustomed to using along other sections of coastline and you'll have little difficulty coaxing strikes from stripers.

Boat fishermen consistently catch stripers trolling, live-bait fishing, casting, and jigging along the entire coast. There is excellent striper sport in the waters of Nantucket and Martha's Vineyard, where we've visited with the *Linda June*. A spot we haven't fished is unquestionably one of Massachusetts's most famous, and that's the tiny island of Cuttyhunk, which is part of the Elizabethan Island chain. It's noted for its super-sized stripers, and one day we'll get there, too.

The Cape Cod Canal, with its swift current, joins Cape Cod Bay with Buzzards Bay. I view it as the longest inlet jetty I've ever fished, all 6 miles of it. The banks of the canal are lined with rock riprap, and the same techniques used on tiny inlet jetties all along the coast work just perfectly in the "Big Ditch." I've fished myself to exhaustion, chasing after bass that surged with a ripping current, as I stumbled over the riprap. Plugs, leadheads, and rigged eels, cast up and across the current and worked through the rips, bring wild strikes in the heavy current.

I've also scored while drifting live mackerel and herring baits from a small boat at either end of the canal. At Sandwich best results are achieved as the tide flows into Cape Cod Bay, while at the west end you want the tide flowing into Buzzards Bay.

Many fond memories drift back of fishing with renowned plug manufacturer Stan Gibbs, whose home was located right on the banks of the canal. Fishing with him from his outboard rig he proved to me, without question, that his wooden plugs, especially the surface swimmer, turned on a lathe in his workshop, were then and continue to be among the finest striper lures ever made. Stan trailered his boat, and within a few minutes' drive of his home knew every launching ramp; he could have his boat in the water and we'd be casting to stripers—sometimes big bluefish, too—in less time than it takes to write this sentence.

The fly caster is also at home all along the Massachusetts coastline. Shore- and boat-based anglers have many protected waters such as Plymouth Bay, Barnstable Harbor, Provincetown, Wellfleet, Pleasant Bay, Chatham, and the broad expanse of Buzzards Bay to try their skills. Saltwater fly fishing in this area has taken on the prominence of fishing the Keys flats for bonefish, with a methodical dedication not found in most other types of striper fishing.

MISSISSIPPI

Much of what I said of the state of Louisiana is equally applicable to Mississippi. Compared with other coastal states, a viable fishery for striped bass does not exist. There are, however, pockets of striped bass found in tributaries of the Mississippi River and some of the impoundments that feed into it. Next to other striped bass fisheries along the coast, Mississippi's fishery does not exist in the sense of providing continuing, stable angling. It has had severe declines in recent years despite the best efforts of state officials to reestablish the fishery through stocking key rivers, of which several flow into the Mississippi River. Historical data indicate that limited populations of striped bass were found in these waters many years ago.

Unfortunately, high nutrient levels as a result of agricultural fertilizer runoff impacts the lower Mississippi and its feeder rivers, which, when combined with periods of high salinity brought about by periodic drought conditions, has all but eliminated what could have been a viable fishery.

NEW HAMPSHIRE

If you're driving too fast along the coastal road you'll pass through New Hampshire before you realize it. While it admittedly has a tiny coastline, there are substantial numbers of stripers available for both beach and boat anglers. By far the best fishing occurs in the Hampton, Oyster, and Piscataqua Rivers, where small-boat anglers regularly score with both lures and natural baits.

Often traveling anglers fail to realize the potential of this tiny piece of coastline, for when they're traveling on Interstate 95 they're through the state in a matter of minutes. It's certainly worth your effort to get off after you cross the Merrimack River and head east a couple of miles to enjoy the pleasant ride north along the old coast road.

There's a type of striper sport to suit every angler. Trailer boatmen can launch in the Hampton River and fish its waters or venture out into Hampton Harbor, where it empties into the ocean. Shore-based anglers will find miles of picturesque beach to cast lures or natural baits to stripers that frequent the area from late spring until autumn northeasters chase them south during October.

NEW JERSEY

I was fortunate enough to catch my first striper in New Jersey, and over many decades have lived in the Garden State and sampled the wide range of striper fishing it has to offer.

Its natural border with New York in the northeastern part of the state is the magnificent Hudson River, second only to the Chesapeake Bay as a prime striper spawning ground. New Jersey has over 125 miles of coastal beaches fronting the Atlantic Ocean, with Raritan Bay to the north and Delaware Bay to the south. In between lie many great striped bass rivers such as the Navesink, Shrewsbury, Shark, Manasquan, Toms, and Mullica, to name but a few.

Stripers are also found in Sandy Hook Bay, Barnegat Bay, Great Bay, and Great Egg Harbor Bay, as well as the myriad small bays and estuaries scattered along the barrier beaches found along much of the south Jersey coast.

There are beaches galore, and groins and jetties, bridges and bulkheads, and fishing piers to accommodate the land-based angler. It's important to note that the surf is public domain up to the high-water mark, and so long as you don't have to cross private property you have access to it. Simply put, you can walk and fish the surf for miles and not be prohibited nor intimidated from doing so.

The same holds true for jetties and groins, which were built with public funds, and easements provided to access them. Some of the most enjoyable striped bass fishing I've ever experienced, and where I've landed many really big bass, has been from the rock piles of Tackanassee, Deal, Elberon, Spring Lake, and Sea Girt. Fishing with jetty jockeys like Charlie Searles, Nat Lane, Tom Fergus, Johnny Celaya, and Johnny Creenan was among the most exciting fishing I've ever done. We are, to many, a motley crew, as we climb around coastal rock piles in the dark of night, dressed in storm gear, cleated soles, and miner's headlamps, casting into a stiff northeast wind. Words can't describe it. You've just got to climb out on a rock pile and try it!

New Jersey's western border is the majestic Delaware Bay, which has a population of striped bass well north to the New York State border. In recent years stripers have expanded their range well up into the upper reaches of this river. I've fished for them a full 175 miles up the river from the ocean, and while still in New Jersey. The reason they've done so well is the huge food source, particularly the massive schools of herring and shad fry that are hatched and spend their early months in the river. The months from early spring until late fall see unlimited opportunities to catch stripers on a wide array of tackle, while both fishing from boats and casting from shore.

All along the seacoast there are marinas that have party and charter boats available to seek stripers from early spring until December's northeasters send them to their winter quarters. One- and two-man guide boats are also available, and are especially popular with fly fishermen.

NEW YORK

New York State has it all when it comes to striper fishing. Over a span of many years the Empire State has seldom, if ever, failed me when I've sought out the prince of the unpreditables. The beautiful South Shore of Long Island has six inlets that empty into the sea: Rockaway, East Rockaway, Jones, Fire Island, Moriches, and Shinnecock. The inlet jetties provide striper sport from early spring until after Thanksgiving. Between these inlets are over 100 miles of beautiful beach, and I doubt there's a square foot of it that doesn't hold a population of stripers from April through year's end during a mild fall. Choose your weapons, for you'll find that casters using lures will score, as will the contemplative angler who sets up and fishes natural baits from the beach.

On my last visit out east a group of us, including Ken Schultz of *Field & Stream* magazine and Wayne Nester of the *Suffolk Sun*, fished with noted surf guides Fred Golofaro and Tommy Melton. Before we left the beach each of us had scored with from 6 to 10 mixed blues and stripers up to 15 pounds on darters cast into the Shagwong Point rips on an ebbing tide. Exciting sport on a dark night with an onshore wind, and some heavy breakers that almost did several members of the party in!

It's easy for boatmen to find exciting fishing in the beautiful barrier island bays, including Jamaica, South Oyster, Great South, Moriches, and Shinnecock Bays. These bays are very shallow, banked with marsh grass and studded with picturesque marsh islands. The water is teeming with grass shrimp and other forage on which the stripers feed throughout the summer, providing great sport for the angler who fishes live bait, chums, drifts and jigs, or casts lures.

On the east end there's Montauk, providing possibly the greatest variety of striper fishing that you could ever ask for. I've made it a ritual to fish Montauk during the fall for many years, as it's then that the fishing borders on the fantastic. An excellent fleet of charter

Party boats are popular on both the Atlantic and Pacific coasts, where anglers regularly score with striped bass. The Lazybones *is drifting off Shagwong Point off Montauk, New York, where many of the anglers on board caught limit catches while vertical jigging.*

boats sails from Montauk Harbor on the North Shore, where it spreads out and you can troll, cast, jig, drift, or fish live baits.

As I was putting the finishing touches on this book, I enjoyed superb sport with big bass while fishing with Captain Steve Witthuhn and mate Pete Kazura on board the *Tophook,* as we jigged parachute jigs and pork rind in the rips just off from the point. My top bass weighed 32 pounds. The next night I boarded the party packet *Sea Otter,* with Captain Joel Lizza and mate Chuck Etzel, and scored with a pair up to 30 pounds while drifting live eels just off Shagwong. I've been doing this out east for more than 40 years, and Montauk just never lets me down.

Each season sees many respectable-sized stripers landed from these waters, as the stripers set up residence to avail themselves of the plentiful supply of forage, including herring, mackerel, menhaden, bay anchovies (popularly called rainfish), mullet, and sand eels. There are six-man charter boats, small two-man charters for light tackle and fly fishing, and a sizable fleet of party boats, all specializing in striper fishing.

The North Shore of Long Island borders on Long Island Sound, and here the angler has a completely different environment from the South Shore. Over 100 miles of shoreline extend to Orient Point and provide casting opportunities, with areas strewn with boulders that bass find to their liking. Boatmen employ a wide array of techniques, including trolling, jigging, and casting, to score.

Moving west, after anglers pass beneath the Throgs Neck bridge there's great fishing, especially during the spring and fall, when migrating stripers move to and from the sound through the East River. The area from Hellgate to the Brooklyn Bridge teems with stripers, plus some big bluefish, and they're caught using every technique discussed in this book. Fishing with Tony DeLernia aboard his *Rocket Charters,* which sails from Manhattan, I've scored while chumming, jigging, and casting until arm-weary.

From the Verrazano Narrows Bridge north there's exciting fishing to be found in New York Harbor, right within the shadow of the Statue of Liberty. To the south, and right around the corner, is famous Coney Island, with fine striper sport on the Coney Island Flats and Tin Can Grounds. It was at the latter spot that Don Bingler designed the famous Bingle Banana, a tube lure for jigging and trolling that stripers can't resist.

The Hudson River is second only to the Chesapeake Bay as a spawning and nursery ground for stripers. Each winter the river hosts a huge population of bass, and many big ones at that. The migration begins in earnest during November, with the fish relatively inactive throughout the winter. After spawning in the spring, the exodus begins in April, as the fish return to sound and ocean waters to spend the summer, most heading north to New England and Canadian waters.

NORTH CAROLINA

North Carolina waters play host to huge schools of striped bass, many traveling to and from the waters of Albemarle Sound. This is their home water, where many of them were born, and it's the third major striped bass spawning and nursery area on the Atlantic coast.

When the striped bass arrive after their summer visit to the waters of New Jersey, New York, and New England, the huge schools provide exciting surf- and boat-fishing opportunities along the Outer Banks. There are times when schools of stripers breaking on bait can be seen for miles on end. Often the air is filled with thousands of gulls dipping and diving to grasp helpless baitfish, as the bass swim through the raging waves crashing across the sandbars to feed.

Casting for these fish from the surf is an exciting challenge, for the Outer Banks have some of the roughest, heaviest surf found anywhere on the Atlantic coast. Distance casting is often a prime consideration, and here the 12-foot-long surf rod, either spinning or conventional, becomes the standard. Often it's necessary to execute 250- to 300-foot long casts to reach feeding stripers; I've frequently used a Hatteras Heaver to reach out to big bass during the early-winter migration. Large Hopkins No-Eql and Shorty hammered stainless-steel jigs, block tin squids with feather or bucktail skirts, and heavy leadhead jigs with soft plastic tails are a must, as it's just impossible to get sufficient distance with lighter lures or tackle.

Boats sailing from Oregon and Hatteras Inlets enjoy superb action, under what at times can be called hazardous conditions, with early-winter wind and waves buffeting them. Trolling produces the best results, with big spoons, plugs, leadhead jigs, and tube lures bringing strikes from very big stripers. This is a time when predominantly female stripers congregate along the Outer Banks, with many fish in the 25- to 50-pound class. Even marine scientists do not fully understand why very few males arrive at this time of the year, and very few of what are commonly referred to as school fish.

It appears that the school stripers, ranging from 6 to 25 pounds, prefer to stay in the waters from Virginia Beach, Virginia, through Kitty Hawk, North Carolina, through early winter. During early spring the schools of the large females and school bass often begin to disperse and move toward their home waters in Albemarle Sound, and often moving 100 miles to the west up the Roanoke River near Weldon, North Carolina, a major spring spawning area.

While the big bass seem to travel great distances, there is a huge population of small stripers, ranging from newly hatched fish to those weighing 5 or 6 pounds, that spend the first four or five years of their life right within the confines and many river systems of Currituck, Albemarle, and Pamlico Sounds.

These fish provide exciting fishing for the relatively small group of anglers who seek them. The area of sound and river waters inside the Outer Banks barrier islands is immense. I doubt if a person in a lifetime of fishing could ever fish every haunt in the myriad waterways of North Carolina. The majority of the inland fishing is done from small boats, with natural baits such as live shrimp, soft or peeler blue crabs, spot, and mullet being the favorite baits. Light one-handed spinning and popping outfits are favored for casting small plugs and leadhead jigs in the miles of rivers that empty into the three major sounds.

RHODE ISLAND

Looking over some vintage files, I note it was way back in 1961 that Art Lavallee, of Providence, invited me to "come take a crack at Rhode Island stripers anytime." I'd frequently used his Kastmaster metal squids, so the invite was not set aside.

It was shortly after our arrival in the tiny state that I was introduced to its picturesque Narragansett Bay, with stately mansions dotting the shoreline, rocky outcroppings, marsh grass, and striped bass. My expectations were fulfilled, for a bay veteran like Art methodically probed the haunts that consistently produced bass. Some were spots that looked inconsequential, but he knew that where the rip line formed there were sure to be bass, and there were.

What I liked most about fishing the bay, which is a huge body of water for our smallest state, is that it's light-tackle fishing at its finest. I alternated between light spinning popping outfits, and used a wide array of poppers, swimmers, and bucktail jigs. Drifting sandworms also produced well with light gear in spring, and I scored with many nice bass using live eels during the fall migration.

On later junkets I used a fly rod to good advantage, depending almost entirely on the Honey Blonde of Joe Brooks that was so popular in that era. Today the fly casters who fish the bay go forth with the creations of Popovics, Clouser, and Kreh. There are so many creations coming off the bench of fly tiers that they number in the thousands, from tiny red flies that resemble a worm hatch to huge patterns with glued-on eyes that mimic an adult bunker. All will, at one time or another, attract the fancy of a hungry striper. The stripers are plentiful in the upper reaches of the bay from bustling Cranston, through Warwick, and in the many coves and estuaries that feed the bay.

There's also fine fishing out of Point Judith, where trolling, casting, jigging, live-bait fishing, and chumming all provide fine sport off the coast's fewer than 40 miles of seacoast.

Jetty jockeys will just love Charlestown Breachway. When the tide ebbs and feeds a variety of forage into the ocean, the stripers often stack up in the rips and eddies like cordwood, waiting for a meal. While I've scored with heavy bucktail jigs when the tide is boiling, the most exciting action is at the tail end of the ebbs, with the current just sliding along, casting a big wooden surface swimmer out and across the narrow breachway and ever so slowly retrieving it through the swirling rips. The wild surface strikes are guaranteed to get your adrenaline pumping.

Still another fantastic striper haunt of Little Rhody is Block Island. Situated just 10 miles offshore, Block provides every kind of striper sport imaginable. During our last visit with the *Linda June* we were tied to a T dock for several days and I caught winter flounder from our cockpit right at the dock. A walk along the Old Harbor riprap and marshes enabled me to watch stripers searching for a meal in the clear, shallow water along the shoreline, occasionally joined by cruising bluefish. Just observing them was exciting.

While the island is small, there's plenty of beautiful beach, with picturesque bluffs, enabling you to fish in almost any weather—

there's always a lee. Situated as it is, Block Island has a huge commuter population of stripers that go by each spring and fall, resulting in exciting fishing on the tackle of your choice.

OREGON

While Leon Adams has spoken highly of Oregon's limited striped bass fishery, it's one of the few spots that I've yet to seek my favorite game fish. Leon enjoyed fine fishing in the waters of Coos Bay, using much the same techniques he employed in San Francisco Bay, from where the Coos Bay stripers emigrated. The upper reaches of the Coquille regularly produce stripers, but not to the extent of the Umpqua River and its Smith River tributary to the north and the Rogue River to the south, both of which have resident populations of fish that do not appear to migrate in the way that East Coast stripers do.

Most biologists agree that the stocks in the Umpqua and Coquile Rivers come from San Francisco Bay, which is hundreds of miles distant. Little is known of their migration pattern, and there's no specific fishery from the surf of Oregon's coastline for the species.

SOUTH CAROLINA

Almost all of South Carolina's river systems host a population of striped bass. There is very little migration of stripers from these coastal rivers. The most prominent rivers are the Santee and Cooper; their population of stripers is composed both of ocean stocks of the species, and of stocks that enter the rivers upstream from impoundments. Lake Marion is a huge impoundment of 96,400 acres with a perimeter of 315 miles that backs up behind Santee Dam, which empties into the Santee River and ultimately into the ocean. Lake Moultrie's waters consist of 60,300 acres with a perimeter of 135 miles and are held back by Pinopolis Dam, which empties into the Cooper River, which meets the Atlantic at Charleston.

Little did anyone realize back in 1938, when these two gigantic hydroelectric impoundments were built, that they would become home to a huge population of landlocked striped bass that would reproduce naturally within their confines. The result has been a wonderful inland fishery that provides exciting recreational angling all year long.

From this landlocked population literally hundreds of thousands of striped bass fry have been provided to other states to stock impoundments throughout the country. The most notable recipient was Lake Texoma on the border of Texas and Oklahoma, where the population has flourished and provides unbelievable fishing. Many of the more than 20 states that now have landlocked populations of stripers are indebted to South Carolina and the Santee-Cooper stocks.

For dyed-in-the-wool striper fans accustomed to high surf, jetties, boiling tide rips, and rough seas, fishing at Lakes Marion and Moultrie will provide a totally new experience.

The favorite mode of transportation on the lakes is small, trailered outboard boats and pontoon boats up to 26 feet in length. The pontoon boats are especially popular with the guides who fish the lake, and can accommodate up to six anglers aboard a roomy, stable craft.

Especially noteworthy for the traveling fisherman is the fact that South Carolina provides free public launching ramps at strategic locations along the shores of both lakes. In all of my travels along the Atlantic, Pacific, and Gulf coasts I have never seen launching ramps that could compare with those in South Carolina. They were built with excellent engineering, in fine locations, with safety paramount, excellent roadway access to put in and take out, and ample on-site parking for cars and trailers. They're the best.

As you move out onto the lake you'll observe that it's a propeller-repair shop owner's heaven. Tens of thousands of tree stumps were left in place at the time the impoundments were built, so that electric power could be generated by the advent of World War II.

The net result is that the stumps are still there, providing shelter for a wide variety of species found in the impoundments, including not only striped bass but also black crappie, white crappie, largemouth bass, shellcracker, bluegill, channel catfish, blue catfish, and white bass. It's the only place I've fished for stripers and was constantly surprised when a big channel catfish or lunker largemouth bass struck!

The two most popular methods of fishing for stripers in these lakes are with natural baits or while jigging and casting artificials. In isolated spots you can troll, but it's seldom done.

The popping outfit with a small level-wind reel is by far the most popular tackle. The pontoon boats are rigged with rod holders, and the favorite technique is to fish with six lines, sending two baits to the bottom, two to intermediate depths, and livelining the remaining two as the boat drifts along. To slow the drift, especially on windy days, many guides employ a sea anchor, a miniature parachute that slows the drift over choice bottom.

The electronic fishfinder becomes an important tool in the impoundments, for it enables you to move along bottom favored by stripers and not even wet a line until you locate the fish. Often they're on the move, as the schools of herring and gizzard shad on which they feed move about to avoid them. Thus, it becomes a search-and-find mission before the boat is positioned and the baits streamed out.

Because of the tremendous number of bottom obstructions, 20-pound line is the standard. This enables you pull free of the bottom should you become fouled, whereas lighter line results in a great attrition of rigs. The guides also use a stiff wire arm on their bottom rig, which slides over obstructions and prevents the sinker and hook from becoming fouled.

While the baited lines are streaming away from the pontoon boat as you drift along, many anglers pick up a popping outfit and probe the depths with a ¼- or ½-ounce Hopkins or leadhead jig with a soft plastic tail.

There are often occasions when the herring and gizzard shad school on the surface, being chased by stripers from below, just as they do along the seacoast, and this provides exciting casting opportunities. As is the case along the seacoast, the key is positioning the boat so you drift with the fish within casting range and do not spook them by motoring too close.

Your favorite striper lures, including swimming and popping plugs and darters, spoons, small tin squids and jigs, and leadheads, all bring quick strikes when the fish are chasing bait on the surface, often accompanied by the same gulls and terns you're accustomed to seeing in salt water.

When the fish are on top it's a perfect opportunity to use a fly rod. I travel with an 8-weight outfit, and found it ideal when casting to the stripers of Lakes Marion and Moultrie. If the bass aren't showing, I've used a 400-grain tip, which I brought into play as we drifted over stripers that showed up on the fishfinder at intermediate depths. The 400-grain line gets down fast and, when used with a fly like a saltwater Clouser Minnow in blue and white with silver Mylar, or chartreuse and white with silver Mylar, readily brings strikes from stripers feeding on small fry.

I've often used a small Popovics popper when fly casting among the myriad stumps. Just drifting along among the stumps, where the stripers are cruising and looking for a meal, often brings explosive strikes. Use a short leader—6 feet maximum—with at least a 16-pound-test tippet; when you hook fish in the stumps you've got to muscle them in quickly or suffer a cutoff.

The waters of these two impoundments, South Carolina's most famous striper locales, are very similar to what you'll encounter at Lake Texoma and many of the other impoundments throughout the country where stripers have been introduced. Although bass that top 30 pounds are regularly caught, for the most part the recreational angler is dealing with fish from 2 to 10 pounds in weight—ideally suited for light tackle, whether your choice be one-handed spinning, level-wind casting, or fly casting.

TEXAS

There's a saying that has circulated for years that when Texans do something, they do it big. Such was the case when back in 1938 the U.S. Army Corps of Engineers began construction of Denison Dam, forming an impoundment that came to be known as Lake Texoma. The lake borders both Texas and Oklahoma, hence the name. It has 89,000 surface acres of water and 583 miles of shoreline. It's also said to have the largest striped bass population of any inland lake in the world!

I first learned of the fine striped bass fishing in Lake Texoma from Kelwyn Ellis, a fan who read my early exploits on striper fishing back in the 1950s and now lives in Denison, just 10 minutes from terrific fishing for stripers in the impoundment.

It wasn't until 1960 that the state first stocked stripers, which were provided by South Carolina and transplanted from Lakes Marion and Moultrie, discussed at length in the segment on South Carolina. The striped bass thrived and became a self-sustaining, economically vital and valuable resource in the area. Their biologists have documented natural spawning each year for several decades. The high salinity content of the Red and Washita Rivers is no doubt well suited to the stripers, which spawn as though it were their own home.

The Lake Texoma record striper is a 35-pound beauty, but just below Denison Dam a heavyweight of 43½ pounds was landed. It appears that the bass have thrived to the point that they now have colonized every major tributary of the Red River all the way to the Gulf of Mexico. But there their travel ends, as there does not appear to be a migration movement into the Gulf, compared to our East Coast stripers moving into the open ocean.

While you would hardly think there'd be "surf" or "jetty" fishing in an impoundment, Kelwyn likens the fishing he does to just those techniques. He employs standard surf tackle when fishing in the river below the dam, where the swift current and heavy water on windy, stormy days often result in the same effect. Indeed, he asserts that his best catches of big stripers occur at night, attesting to the nocturnal feeding habits of stripers. Much like surf stripers, they respond to the standard plugs, spoons, spinnerbaits, and leadhead jigs. Gizzard shad, threadfin shad, and ghost minnows are all popular hook baits and constitute the major forage on which stripers feed in both the lake and entire river system.

In the lake proper, Kelwyn has a few favorite spots around boat ramps, usually deserted at night, during the early morning and especially on windy days, when people often don't venture onto the lake. The only difference is that when windswept water crashes across the rocks and showers you, it doesn't taste like salt!

While the one-handed spinning outfit and light level-wind casting outfit are the tackle of choice of lake anglers, fly fishing has come into vogue in recent years. Casting to stripers in the big lake and the many rivers isn't much different from fishing in bays and rivers along the coast.

Especially exciting is when the stripers are schooling and chasing shad and minnows on the surface, which presents great opportunities for fly casters—a 50- or 60-foot cast from a drifting boat places your fly in the midst of the feeding fish. It's always best to carry a sinking line, too, because when the fish are in the depths and show up on your fishfinder, it's relatively easy to get down to them with a 400-plus-grain fly line or a fly line with a lead-core shooting head. As along the coast, the Clouser Flashtail and Lefty's Deceivers are popular, as are the Glazener Spinster and Blanton's Flashtail Whistlers. Most patterns are tied on 3/0 hooks and range in length from 2 to 5 inches. Favorite color combinations include chartreuse and white, chartreuse and gray, yellow and red, and blue and white. Add a trace of Mylar, either gold or silver, to give the fly sparkle.

The beauty of fishing Lake Texoma is that good fishing is available all year long. For a lake that has the largest inland striped bass population in the world, there are always a few willing to cooperate somewhere along its 583-mile shoreline.

VIRGINIA

Virginia's another state that's got it all when it comes to striped bass fishing. The Eastern Shore stretching from Ocean City to Cape Charles has magnificent beaches from which migrating stripers are caught by surfmen. Ocean City's inlet provides jetty jockeys with dexterity the opportunity to cast their leadhead jigs to productive water on an ebbing tide. The city's marinas have fine fleets of charter and party boats to capitalize on the striper's migrations each spring and fall. The fishing is typical of what you'd find along the Northeast coast, as are the techniques used to catch stripers.

Importantly, Virginia's got the Chesapeake Bay, too, which is the largest nursery grounds for striped bass in the country. As I prepare this text many names come to mind, including Saxis, Crisfield, Chesapeake Beach, the James and York Rivers, and the Rappahannock. Visiting each of these spots was initially a challenge, but soon after arriving and fishing with natives like Joe Sparrow and Claude Rogers many years ago, I fell into their pattern of fishing, and often caught stripers until I was arm-weary. These spots are a striped bass haven, with mile upon mile of beautiful marsh banks, forage beyond description, and hungry, cooperative stripers.

It's important to note that not too many years ago the Chesapeake Bay, along with many other waterways that the striped bass call home, was being negatively impacted by pollution. Fortunately, the actions of state and federal officials have made tremendous progress in preventing pollution, and as a result the water quality—and the quality of the fishing—has improved markedly.

All of these spots, which are only a tiny fraction of hundreds of excellent fishing locales on the Chesapeake Bay and its tributary rivers and creeks, are the nursery grounds for stripers that range all the way to Canada's Maritime provinces. Many of the fish spend several years in the bay. When they reach 4 to 6 pounds in weight they get the urge, for whatever reason, to travel, and they join others in a migration trek each spring and fall.

There's a method of striper fishing on the broad expanse of the Chesapeake to satisfy everyone's needs. It's a paradise for small-boat anglers, who regularly troll its productive waters. Chumming is very popular, with grass shrimp by far the most popular chum, although recent years have seen the growing popularity of chunks of menhaden or clam bellies as chum, all with fine results. Casters, including fly fishermen, delight in presenting their lures to feeding stripers when the bass are on top chasing bait, as is often the case when huge schools of baby bunker move out of creeks and estuaries into the open bay, where the schools number in the thousands, with a constant onslaught from the stripers. Marine scientists are quick to emphasize the importance of menhaden to the striped bass fishery in the Chesapeake—they are the major forage species on which stripers feed.

The lower bay has the engineering marvel known as the Chesapeake Bay Bridge and Tunnel complex, joining Cape Charles with Virginia Beach. Here boatmen troll, anchor up and chum, drift and jig, stem the tide and cast to the riprap, or fish the shadow lines of the two bridges with light casting tackle. It's extraordinary fishing, with a fine fleet of charter and party boats available at Virginia Beach.

It's important to note that all of the river systems throughout the state hold stripers, as well as the open bay, and almost every waterfront community has its local marina and tackle shops that are pleased to dispense information to visiting fishermen. This is the beginning of the South, where hospitality reigns supreme, and visitors are always welcome, especially striped bass fishermen.

WASHINGTON

You'd think that with stripers having so well adapted to the San Francisco Bay, they'd expand their range along the entire Northwest coast and provide fine fishing to Washington anglers. While this is true in the Northeast, where anglers enjoy superb striper fishing in Maine, such is not the case in Washington State.

Stripers are found in the Columbia River, which forms a natural border between Washington and Oregon, and they also frequent several other river systems along the coast, but in very sparse numbers. The quantity of bass found in these waters is rather limited, and as a result anglers concentrate their efforts on the more plentiful salmon and other species.

CANADA'S MARITIME PROVINCES

Striped bass regularly cross the border from the U.S. into Canada, where many have established permanent residence in the river systems of New Brunswick, Newfoundland, and Nova Scotia and the St. Lawrence Seaway. While I have not fished the Maritime provinces for striped bass, I've spoken with several anglers who have.

It appears that when Atlantic coast striped bass populations are at their peak, stripers move farther north in search of food, and on arriving along the Canadian coast move inland into the numerous river systems where forage such as sand eels, herring, and mackerel are extremely plentiful.

In the early 20th century there were numerous local populations of striped bass that spawned in the rivers. With industrialization and the building of dams across their spawning grounds, the populations simply disappeared. With removal of some dams in recent years, though, there have been signs that some stripers have again begun to move to the headwaters of the rivers to spawn. Unfortunately, the fishery that exists is not one where even native anglers can predict with any certainty as to the movements, let alone the catchability of stripers on a consistent basis.

AMERICA'S INLAND LAKES

As I began to prepare this final segment on America's inland lakes, I thought a compilation of all lakes in which stripers are found would be appropriate. I quickly realized such a listing would really serve no more purpose than if I were to list every sound, bay, or river in which stripers are found along the seacoast.

The phenomenon that has taken place with striped bass successfully being stocked in freshwater lakes and impoundments is nothing short of a miracle. Some stockings have resulted in the species thriving in the waterway into which it is introduced, where moving river waters enabled bass to successfully spawn and reproduce.

But a failure to reproduce has prevented the fishery from developing in lakes that are not fed by moving river waters. This has resulted in regular stocking programs of hatchery-reared fingerling stripers. In most instances, however, the bass have thrived, in great part as a result of biologists benefiting from years of experience at stocking—sometimes failing, but most often succeeding, in introducing the striped bass to more waters. At last count the striper was thriving in the fresh waters of more than 20 inland states.

In lakes where the transplanted fish haven't taken hold and reproduced, many state fish and game departments have taken to stocking hybrid stripers. The hybrid is bred from striped bass and white bass, and when hatchery-reared to fingerling size adapts to a wide range of water conditions. Given time, I suspect that the striper, along with the hybrid striper, will have been introduced and become a significant factor in providing recreational angling opportunities to anglers the length and breadth of the contiguous United States.

I think it is fair to say that many of the techniques discussed throughout this book have application in the inland striped bass fishery. Granted, the ocean fishery is often for bigger fish under more demanding conditions, but the basic approach—casting, jigging, drifting, using natural baits, or trolling—proves just as successful. The key is balancing the tackle to the available fishery, maximizing the contemplative, most enjoyable sport of catching the "king of the surf" in a freshwater environment.

More than a score of inland states host striped bass in their impoundments, lakes, and rivers. The bass provide light-tackle fishing at its finest, with a stable pontoon boat the favorite fishing craft on the big lakes.

In Conclusion

If you've read this far, I suspect one of two things will happen. You will have determined that this thing called "striped bass fishing" is just too much for you. Rising hours before first light to be on the beach when the stripers turn on, or probing the darkness to find a rip line where old linesides may be feeding may just not be what excites you.

Then again, watching the sun lift off the horizon may be something you've experienced for the first time now that you've begun to seek the princely striper. Couple this with the experience of watching shooting stars tumble from the skies on a night tide when a million other stars held you in awe and you've come to realize that striped bass fishing is a lot more than just catching.

Donning a bathing suit to rake calico crabs in the surf, or throwing a cast net to obtain mullet, or simply jigging mackerel for live baits is every bit as much a part of striper fishing as the actual catching.

So is the excitement that fills the air as terns and gannets scream and dive while stripers chase baitfish from below. I still remember a red fox that stalked me on a barrier beach, wondering why I invaded its domain just before daybreak a few days before I penned this conclusion. I'll never forget the cry of a loon, heard while casting a plug at night to a rip on a placid coastal bay. I get goose bumps even as I write about hearing that cry.

Then there are the exciting times—stemming the tide as a roaring rip line churns off your stern, say, with the strike of a big striper bringing you to your knees at the transom. The taste of salt water as a roaring northeaster crashes waves against a coastal jetty and line screams from your reel while a bass heads into those awesome waves . . . it's all what striper fishing is about.

Of all the words used to describe striped bass fishing, I always come back to the word *contemplative*. To me it's the word that best describes fishing for striped bass. Believe me when I say it's not the

Left: Memories are made of this.

catching that has held me spellbound these many years. It's the total experience: choosing the tackle, rising early, persevering despite heat, cold, wind, rain. Importantly, enjoying the bounty of nature, the beauty of the outdoors. It's something that many people never get to experience, but that June and I have enjoyed for a lifetime. It's contemplative, and should never be competitive.

Join us and I promise you'll never regret the challenge of one day calling yourself a striped bass angler. It's a title I love and will always cherish.

Index